BLUEHOUSE

藍房子

Blue House

Bei Dao

Translated from the Chinese by
Ted Huters and
Feng-ying Ming

ZEPHYR PRESS
BROOKLINE, MASSACHUSETTS

Publication was assisted by a grant from
The Massachusetts Cultural Council.

Cover and book design by typeslowly
Photos throughout *Blue House* appear courtesy of Bei Dao
Printed by McNaughton & Gunn

Library of Congress Control Number: 00 136017
ISBN 0-939010-58-5

FIRST EDITION
ZEPHYR PRESS
50 KENWOOD STREET   BROOKLINE, MA 02446
www.zephyrpress.org

Grateful acknowledgment is made to the following:

"Howl" by Allen Ginsberg, from COLLECTED POEMS, copyright © 1988, Reprinted by permission of HarperCollins.

"The Street" by Octavio Paz, translated by Muriel Rukeyser, from EARLY POEMS OF OCTAVIO PAZ, copyright © 1973 by Octavio Paz and Muriel Rukeyser, Reprinted by permission of New Directions Publishing Corp.

"Streets in Shanghai" by Tomas Tranströmer, translated by Robin Fulton, from NEW COLLECTED POEMS, copyright © 1987, 1997 by Robin Fulton and Bloodaxe Books, Reprinted by permission of Bloodaxe Books.

"Trilce LXXV" by César Vallejo, translated by Clayton Eshleman, from TRILCE, copyright © 2000 by Clayton Eshleman and Wesleyan University Press, Reprinted by permission of Wesleyan University Press.

Blue House originally published as:

國家圖書館出版品預行編目資料

　藍房子 = Blue house / 北島著. --初版. --
　臺北市：九歌，民 87
　　面：　　公分.--（九歌文庫：518）
　ISBN　957-560-568-3(平裝)

87013591

CONTENTS

PUBLISHER'S NOTE

Several essays from the original version of *Lan Fangzi* (*Blue House*) were excised by the author and the editorial board of Zephyr Press. Revisions were then made to a few of the remaining essays after completion of the initial translation. These revisions were done in conjunction with Bei Dao, and focused primarily on emending some facts, and removing biographical information for individuals and locations already familiar to the the book's new audience.

Zephyr Press would like to thank Bei Dao, Clayton and Caryl Eshleman, John and Ann Rosenwald, Gary Snyder, and Eliot Weinberger for their editorial comments on various essays. Zephyr would also like to thank Kathy Lu — spark for the entire project.

ALLEN GINSBERG IN SEOUL, KOREA (AUGUST, 1990)

ALLEN GINSBERG

"Check out this suit, five bucks; leather shoes, three bucks; shirt, two bucks; tie, one dollar — all of it secondhand. Only my poetry is firsthand." Allen once boasted.

I met Allen Ginsberg in 1983, when he came to China as part of a group of American authors. My English translator, Bonnie McDougall, had arranged for me to meet him and his comrade in arms, Gary Snyder. We met secretly in Allen's hotel room, as I was, at that time, a "problematical person" and a key target in the government's *Anti-Spiritual Pollution Campaign*. I had recently been told to take some time off from work and "reflect."

During our first meeting I wasn't overly impressed with either of them. They didn't know much about contemporary Chinese poetry and the only thing they seemed truly interested in was my dissident status.

The next time I saw Allen was five years later in New York at a Chinese poetry festival he had organized. As soon as we arrived, Allen invited Shao Fei, my wife, and me to dinner at a Japanese restaurant. A mutual friend hissed across the table in Chinese, "make sure the penny pinching Jew picks up the tab." At the time I had no idea what he could possibly have against Allen, who willingly picked up the check, gave me a secondhand tie as a memento, and was extremely gracious throughout dinner. It was obvious that he had paid absolutely no attention to Shao Fei during dinner, but that seemed like a fairly minor offense.

The sponsor of the poetry festival was New York's Shower Curtain Queen — an obese and arrogant old woman who moved sluggishly, but with a great deal of style. It was rumored that many of Allen's expenses were pulled out from behind her curtains. Allen followed behind her like a humble servant, his head bent low — occasionally looking up and winking. His "humility" amazed me.

From that point on we saw each other more frequently. In the summer of 1990, we both attended the World Poetry Congress in Seoul. Well-dressed as usual in only the finest of secondhand clothes, he questioned South Korean officials about the release of political prisoners and Korea's human rights record. The organizers of the festival were upset, but unable to do anything because of Allen's celebrity status. At the banquet, the highest of officials and lowliest of interns pushed their way into photos with him. Allen always dragged me along, despite my protests. I had never seen him as angry as when one of the officials, seeing that I was sharing in Allen's limelight, shoved me out of the way. Allen stomped his feet and exploded: "You son of a bitch! Don't you fucking know he's a friend of mine — a Chinese poet!?" The official quickly apologized and, much to my embarrassment, pushed me back into the line of photos. Every time a similar situation arose later, I always made myself scarce.

When I asked Allen at the Congress why he always wore a tie, he answered that he often needed to speak with politicians concerning human rights, and then added slyly, "And my boyfriend's parents wouldn't like me without a tie."

Not much was happening at the Seoul festival, so Allen and I occasionally snuck out. Like a spy of sorts, he relentlessly snapped photos with his miniature camera. He aimed at people's feet, at the crows on branches, or at the sticky cockroach tape being sold by vendors. While resting by the side of the road, he began to teach me how to meditate. As a Tibetan Buddhist, his greatest wish was one day to make the pilgrimage to Tibet. Whenever we got hungry, we ducked into a small café and sampled the local delicacies. One time when we asked for some tea in a Korean café no one seemed to understand what we wanted. Since some Koreans understand written Chinese, I traced the character "tea" on the table with my finger. The owner nodded and hurried over to the phone. I stopped him before he picked up the receiver, wondering what tea drinking had to do with phone calls. I was afraid he had misunderstood me and was ordering girls. Since we really were thirsty, I mimed drinking tea, and the owner again picked up the phone. We were so flustered by this time that we ended up dashing out of the café.

One evening we wandered into a nightclub downtown where the girls wouldn't let go of Allen. Ten minutes later he finally dragged me out sputtering, "I suppose I should have just told them I'm gay." Back on the street a group of American students spotted Allen, and one shouted, "Hey, aren't you Allen Ginsberg?" "Yes I am," he answered, then added, "You know any good gay clubs around here?" The group burst out laughing. One of them pointed down a street to a club, but I made it clear that I wasn't going in with him. Unsure of what to do, he stood in front of the entrance for several moments and eventually left with me.

Allen was given to fits of nostalgia. In his small New York apartment, he played me a recording of his conversations with Kerouac. Looking forlorn, he talked to me about friendship, arguments, death. "So many of my friends have died from drugs or alcohol." He sighed. I told him that in our twenties, my friends and I consumed *On the Road*. We could recite entire pages. I was genuinely moved by his ability to live in apparent communion with the dead, continuing dialogues from years ago. I pictured him sitting alone at home, listening to the recordings over and over until dusk crept in through the window.

All of these past experiences had convinced Allen to give up smoking and drinking. And apart from the occasional boyfriend, he lived the life of an ascetic. Allen was a workaholic. When at one point he had to hire three and a half secretaries to handle his frenetic schedule, Allen quipped, "I need to keep busy, or else who'd feed them?" Sheer capitalistic logic. He told me that his generous salary as a tenured professor at Brooklyn College made up only a third of his total income. The second third came from royalties and readings, and the remainder from his photography. "I am Allen's head," complained Bob, his longest-lasting secretary. "He drops promises all over the world and forgets. I'm the one who cleans up after him."

The pride and raw strength of his younger days remained evident throughout his later poetry readings. Allen's is poetry to be read aloud — with no silence. At a festival in New Jersey, he read several of my poems in English translation. After scribbling notations all over the page and rearranging the order of various lines, he ascended the podium and began screaming away like a runaway engine pointed straight for the audience. I was left behind like a lost soul, and never again dared invite him to read my poems.

Suffering from heart disease and diabetes, he celebrated his seventieth birthday in 1996. The doctor advised him not to travel. He told me over the phone that lately he'd been dreaming about his dead friends. They were discussing death. He was aging. "I saw the best minds of my generation destroyed by madness…"

II

The day I received the phone call about Allen's death, I shut myself up in my room — a complete blank. That evening I called Gary Snyder. He calmly told me about Allen's last few days in the hospital. The doctors had diagnosed it as liver cancer and given him three to five months. "Man, this means goodbye," Allen told Gary on the phone.

I remember asking Allen whether he believed in reincarnation. His answer was ambiguous, leaning towards disbelief. Snyder had convinced him to join the Tibetan Buddhists; Oriental religion seemed to calm the torture in his soul, as though defusing a bomb. There was a Tibetan mandala on his wall, he had studied under a lama, and he attended meditation retreats in Michigan every year. Unlike Gary, his belief did not come from inner reflection, but was self-imposed from the external world. The Zen Center where he practiced was not far from where I used to live. He would call me from there and ask me to come over, or else he would sneak out to see me. I dubbed him our "wild monk."

In the Ann Arbor Zen Center, the resident Rinpoche was a cousin of the Dalai Lama. Allen studied under this lama, who had been repeatedly criticized by other lamas for his liberal views on the "good life," including sexual liberty. His unconventional teachings seemed to suit Allen just fine.

I visited the center for the first time when Allen invited me to attend one of the Rinpoche's talks. The temple was an ordinary apartment rearranged to look like a meditation center. It was decorated simply with cushions scattered across the floor. Since Allen was the guest of honor, and I was Allen's guest, we had prominent seats on the floor. Most of the forty or so participants were Caucasians from various walks of life. The Rinpoche, who had a square head, fleshy ears, and a placid face, introduced Allen and me to the gathering and then began to teach. He offered oriental wisdom and simple ethics in a sensible, accessible, and engaging way. Allen sat attentively, his eyes lowered.

Eastern religions can exact a profoundly calming effect. What a Western rebel like Allen apparently needed was a spiritual, non-Christian force to help him challenge conventions. Of all the Eastern religions Allen chose one based in the magical, thus aligning himself with a vast and mysterious land and culture filled with the promise of rebirth.

Allen's eyes betrayed his true madness; his eyeballs bulging out at two different angles. He would look at you with one eye and follow his own thoughts with the other. He once gave me a book of his photographs. These black-and-white shots conveyed the twin exposures of his two eyes. Most of the photos were of friends from the Beat Generation huddling together, arms around each other, hanging out with weary smiles. At the very moment that Allen wanted to capture something his focus would drift, like the other eye immersed in the depth of his thoughts. The voice was soft and low, the colors completely faded, because Allen wanted us to experience the power of loss — genuine sadness. Another photo was Allen's self-portrait — sitting naked, legs crossed, facing the bathroom mirror, camera resting in his crotch. His bald head with thick tufts curling up the sides, his eyes flashing like bulbs. The photo must date from at least twenty years back. Was he capturing himself or his own impending sense of loss?

Allen taught me how to take photos. In Seoul in 1990, he teased me about my instant camera. "Dummy cameras make dummies." He advised me to get a miniature manual Olympus like his — small, lightweight, easy to handle, and with excellent manual controls for creating special effects. Unfortunately, this particular brand, since it had been discontinued, could only be bought in secondhand stores. He warned me against using flash, which would destroy the sense of space, and suggested I invest in high-speed film that would do well in lower levels of light. When we met again the following spring, I came equipped with the camera he had suggested. Allen turned it over in his hands, inquired about the exact details of my purchase, and finally agreed that I had gotten a good deal. Then he showed me how to use available light, and how, when the lighting was poor, to press one's arms against the chest, and holding one's breath, snap! Snap! — he took two rapid fire pictures of me.

Allen had always taken care of his poorer buddies from the Beat Generation. They said he supported Gregory Corso for years by buying his paintings and giving him spending money. I met Corso once in Allen's apartment. Before he arrived, Allen, beaming with pride, showed me his friend's paintings. Corso turned out to be a husky fellow who dressed like a construction worker. We were sipping tea when Allen suddenly produced a collection of my poems, and Corso, equally unexpectedly, asked me to read one. Corso grunted in appreciation. Allen sat in silence — a mute witness. Then he took us to an Italian restaurant. When Corso asked him for some money to buy cigarettes, Allen tagged along like a skeptical father to make sure he wasn't going to spend it on drugs.

Allen highly recommended Corso's poetry and suggested that I translate him into Chinese. He took me to a bookstore for a copy of Corso's *Mindfield* and then selected the poems he considered particularly significant. I translated a few of these with a friend, and then published them in the journal *Today*. Allen was thrilled, and asked me to mail him a copy immediately so that he could give it to Corso.

Allen often got recognized out on the street. People sometimes dashed into a nearby bookstore to buy a copy of one of his books for him to sign. Time permitting, Allen sketched out a Buddha surrounded by stars and divine creatures with the word "Ha!" coming out of his mouth. Prayer or anger? "I've signed too many things," Allen told me. "Once I'm dead, you'd think they should be worth at least a couple bucks each?"

Two years ago, Allen sold his archives to Stanford for the tidy sum of one million dollars, which created quite a stir. Sheet per sheet Allen figured out that it only averaged about one dollar. After taxes, the amount shrank to six hundred thousand, with which he intended to buy a larger apartment to share with his stepmother.

Allen once organized a fund-raising poetry reading at the Zen Center in Ann Arbor and all four thousand tickets sold out immediately. This gave me the courage to ask if he would help out our journal, *Today*, especially since he was a board member and *Today* was deep in the red. He accepted without a moment's hesitation and suggested that in addition to Gary Snyder, he would include Lawrence Ferlinghetti and Michael McClure. The reading was scheduled for October of 1997, when the Beats were to gather in San Francisco for their fortieth anniversary. Since Allen had fallen ill and could no longer travel without his doctor's approval, Gary Snyder apologized on his behalf and told me that the doctor's prognosis was extremely discouraging. Allen could die at any moment.

Allen and I were day and night — from vastly different geographies and tastes in poetry. He once told me that he didn't understand my later poems, and I felt exactly the same way about his work. I simply had no concept of what he was writing about in his later poetry, but this never hindered our friendship. What I admired most was the way his satirical way would occasionally slip amidst his uncompromising stance against authority. Allen made it considerably easier for everyone who came after him.

He once let me have a look at his just-released FBI dossier. Allen had been on the list of every single administration for fifty years. He had forged ahead like a pawn past the point of no return, seemingly single handedly challenging each heavily guarded king. It had all lasted a full half-century, and for Allen, the confrontation itself was the victory.

III

Now wandering alone, glass in hand through the great halls of New York's Lincoln Center, I am here to attend the benefit dinner honoring the seventy-fifth anniversary of the founding of the American PEN Center. Allen died nine days ago and his name is still on the guest list. I don't know many people here and I have no desire to meet anyone new. I'm searching for Allen in the crowd.

ALLEN GINSBERG AT THE WORLD POETRY CONGRESS IN KOREA (AUGUST, 1990)

Death of a Poet

Allen Ginsberg died April 5, 1997, the day of the Qingming festival in China. I heard later that he had already fallen into a coma, and that his sickroom was filled with friends drinking, talking, and creating a tremendous uproar; none of them acting a bit mournful.

This carefully constructed atmosphere was designed to diminish Allen's feelings of loneliness as he faced death: if life is a party, then there have to be some who arrive late and leave early. Just as the get-together was reaching its peak, Allen wordlessly took his leave. I expected Allen's soul would be somehow unique: perhaps a hissing green flame whistling shrilly as it departed.

One of his line's in its Chinese version came to me: *Women, hold tight to your skirts and prepare for a journey to hell . . . .*

Today is the first anniversary of Allen's death.

I am passing through New York City on my way to a reading upstate. The sun shines radiantly, and I can hear birds call through the buzz of the traffic. I pass though Times Square, continue along Fourteenth Street, then turn onto Third Avenue. This is a New York without Allen.

The pedestrians are stopped at a red light. Their skin color, age, and sex all differ, but their eyes all share the same gaze: impatient, empty, not glancing to the side. Occasionally you see someone gawking around, but they're inevitably visiting, like me.

The light turns green and everyone rushes off; the dogs have to work to keep up. Allen's poems use this New York rhythm; he is a furious shuttle, weaving everything mobile and all that flashes by into lines of poetry. It has now finally come to rest. People have put the shuttle in the drawer and nailed it down. It is a time that no longer needs poetry, and for many years his anger seemed an excess, eventually even growing into a bit of an embarrassment. Gary Snyder speculated to me that on the day Ginsberg died, the media, who customarily paid no attention to him, would suddenly become attentive. And sure enough it happened, and in this case the media was in accord with the mind of the populace: Americans commemorating the departed prefer to forget the past.

When I lived in Ann Arbor Allen often called in the middle of the night and announced in a hoarse voice: "This is Allen." He talked to me about any number of things, about his dreams, his recent travels, or his boyfriends. We didn't run in the same circles so it was safe for him to talk to me.

One day he left a message on my answering machine in a demoralized voice. A Chinese man living in Boston, who had been beaten by his colleagues, had taken the case to Allen, the judge. Allen was given a detailed report: a bloody nose and a swollen face.

"Why would they beat him until he was black and blue?" he roared into the phone, as if he were about to make a formal statement on the state of beatings, after which the media would beat itself bloody and swollen. "Why a bloody nose and swollen face?" he asked again. I tried to explain to him the background of the incident so that he might understand, but it was to no avail. He never could get events straight among us Chinese.

Allen once had a Chinese boyfriend, a young man from Yunnan who used a pen name. I met him at Allen's place. He was small of stature and extremely astute; he had written to introduce himself to Allen while still a student of English in a Chinese university. Allen told me a long time ago that he'd always wanted to support a young man from China to come to New York to study. I remember being puzzled at the time as to where this extraordinary spirit of benevolence had come from. As soon as the young man arrived he moved into Allen's house and began to manage the house, cook, and at the same time serve as his private secretary. Allen was delighted: he could have Chinese food every day without having to go out to eat. The day I visited Allen I saw how deftly the young man functioned, throwing a substantial meal together in no time at all. Allen also treated him very well, putting him on salary in addition to paying his tuition.

A few years later the young man, having scraped together sufficient funds, returned to China to get married. Allen told me that the young man was bisexual, smiled surreptitiously, and said: "He wanted to try a bit of everything."

When Allen got older, all he could do was trust chance, and his readings provided him with good opportunities. When he was shouting out his poems you could be pretty sure that his eyes were never idle, but rather roving about the room in search of prey. After readings, when he was selling and signing books, he'd strike up conversations and most of the time end up hooking someone. The information and discriminatory system within the gay community is no doubt fairly standard, and is dependent upon meaningful glances. A young man waiting for an autograph once told Allen that he also wrote poetry. "Great — come over when you have the time and I'll help you with your poems." But the poems were terrible, completely hopeless. When he had gotten through a few of the poems, Allen sighed: "He's just too young, only nineteen." I could sense the feeling of regret in his voice.

There are two biographies of Allen on the market. He said that one of them is written from a Marxist perspective and the other is Freudian. I asked him what he thought of them. He shook his head, "They're interesting, but neither one is me."

I never asked Allen about his private life, but when he told me about it I listened. One night Kerouac was drunk and got into a brawl at Allen's place, attacking the other guests. After he had endured all he could, Allen threw him out. Kerouac then began to pound on the door and scream, provoking the complaints of the neighbors. When Allen let him in again, he went even more crazy . . . "that was a real catastrophe," sighed Allen. That night was a scar that would not heal for the rest of his life.

The living and the dead invariably have a complicated relationship. Allen and I were not the closest of friends, but after he died I could not banish his image from my mind. Death is like waiting in line, with Allen at the front, his big head bobbing up and down; he suddenly turns around and winks at me. I remember when Allen came to Ann Arbor to see me and embraced me at the door of my house, kissing me fervently on the cheek with his big moist lips. Li Dian, who was standing beside me, was amazed, and elbowed me in the side: "Has the old man fallen for you?"

In the fall of 1993, I went to Eastern Michigan University as a visiting professor in the English Department. At the time

I had just come over from Europe and my English was halting, such that I really could only listen to lectures, not give them. A silent professor! The only thing I could do was organize a poetry reading for the university. I asked Allen for his support and he agreed at once. This was the equivalent of inviting a god down to earth and his response left the abbot of this little temple ecstatic. But our funding was limited and Allen's price for a reading was astronomical. Allen was completely direct: "For a friend, I will do this for nothing." Bob, his secretary, snorted in anger and muttered: "He failed to get my OK."

The auditorium was so packed that many people had to sit in the aisles. Allen was in top form and his voice had ten times the volume of mine; he didn't really need a microphone. Allen's witty obscenities had all the students in stitches. His poetry had become far more concerned with bodily organs than political matters. At the conclusion of the reading, in the manner of the brotherhood of the Chinese greenwood, both of us raised our arms in gestures of respect for the audience.

Summer, 1990, Seoul. At our morning meeting Allen took me aside and enjoined me not to go out that evening, as someone was coming to pick us up, and the Russian poet Voznesensky would be coming along as well. "Remember, don't tell anyone"; he put his index finger to his thick lips.

Allen had amassed decades of experience in the underground struggle, and was thus able to cleverly avoid detection, leading Voznesensky and me to a waiting car. A middle-aged man greeted us. We left the city and went into the surrounding mountains. The roadside became increasingly desolate until we eventually reached a dimly lit residential area, where a group of chattering children led us into a yard on a nearby hillside. In response to the piercing call of a woman's voice, a shadow emerged and put his hands together in greeting. According to the middle-aged man's introduction, this was Korea's most eminent extra-monastic monk.

Three traitors to their superpower nations — add in a wild Korean monk — gathered in an attempt to prove that all men are indeed brothers.

The members of the monk's family set up a small table in the yard and brought out our dinner, which included homemade rice wine. We sat on the ground and the middle-aged man translated. The swarthy monk was as sturdy as a woodcutter. He had never read the sutras and had taken a wife and had children. He was an accomplished poet and painter, and had written quite a few books. And he was crazed enough that he had done a number of paintings with the brush tied onto his member. Allen, who ordinarily didn't touch wine, drained his glass along with the rest of us.

Voznesensky had begun to grow a bit pudgy and was always laughing, quite at odds with what I had imagined of the

21

sharp and angry Russian poet of the *Thaw*. We sat beneath the bright moon and sparse stars, the wine going around several times. We talked of many things, from ancient Chinese poetry to the Korean political situation.

On the way back to the hotel, Allen did not seem to be tired at all, talking the entire way about the wild monk. This was the sort of person he was: whoever was unable to get along with the authorities, startled and resisted the world, grew six fingers, or even ended up with a bloody nose and a swollen face was going to be his friend. This was probably the reason behind our secret meeting in Beijing fifteen years ago.

Allen's greatest wish before he died was to visit Tibet. He planned the trip for years, finally set the date for the summer of 1996, and headed off to Lhasa with a tour group. At the beginning of that year, as he was going on to me about the plans, he told me that he had decided that after Tibet he wanted to visit Beijing and Shanghai in secret. He asked if I could arrange meetings for him with young poets. Not long thereafter he became sick and death confiscated his plans.

The death of a poet does not add or subtract anything from this earth: however unsightly his gravestone might be, however much his books may pollute, however much his gritty spirit may secretly impede the normal operation of the vast mechanism itself.

KOREAN MONK SEATED TO GINSBERG'S LEFT, AND ANDREI VOZNESENSKY, DRESSED ALL
IN WHITE, SEATED DIRECTLY ACROSS FROM GINSBERG

Gary invited me to speak in his creative writing class. He told me that, weather permitting, he almost always held classes outdoors. We walked to a lawn in the Davis Botanical Garden where the students set up two tables. It all looked like a picnic, but we were devouring poetry. Gary sat in the middle, asking who had written a poem recently. Everyone looked around at one another until a girl finally raised her hand and began to recite, the tension registering in her voice. A love poem, written to her lover's eyes. Gary closed his eyes and listened intently, then asked the girl to recite it again. Having received this encouragement, she took a deep breath, unfolded her voice, and this time got completely caught up. Gary nodded his head and made a short critique. It was my turn next.

In teaching creative writing Gary tends toward an Eastern style of imparting information between teacher and student. And as this master happens to be a university professor, his students are probably on the right track. I don't know how many students actually seek out a teacher under the guidance of this sort of obscure Eastern impulse, but I doubt very many. And universities are universities and, according to Ginsberg's rather extreme view, their only function is to "categorize." Gary's take on it is, "Of course you can't teach inspiration in college," preferring that students go into the mountains with him in the summer to work and gain their inspiration from that.

Gary has a face that is hard to forget: deep lines that are essentially all vertical, carved by the hot sun and winter rains. If he doesn't smile, peoples' general impression of him is that he is severe. He loves to smile, however, and his smiles take on the lengthwise wrinkles, linking them all and transforming him into a kindly grandfather. His eyes are always narrowed, as if intentionally hiding from view the light in them; forever gazing into the distance, like a sailor or a forest ranger.

Gary's personality is the exact opposite of Allen's. Allen was unbridled, headstrong, and active as fire. Gary is reserved, tolerant, and with an intuitive wisdom like water. In principle, fire and water cannot abide one another, but despite this they became and remained best of friends for almost half a century.

A mutual friend at one point suggested that beneath Gary's placid exterior must lie a certain turmoil, which can be assumed from his marital history. Gary has been married three times; his first wife was an American and his other two wives were both Japanese. His current wife's family has already been in the the U.S. for three generations; her grandfather brought Japanese rice to California along with his Japanese heritage. Gary and Carole have also adopted a Korean girl who is the same age as my daughter.

Gary told me about the first time he ever met Allen at a bicycle shop on the Berkeley campus in the early 50s. He was putting air in a tire when Allen came over and introduced himself. Figuring back, they must have been in their early twenties, and it was still before the advent of the Beat Generation.

Whenever Allen talked about the beginning of the Beats and the October 1955 reading at the 6 Gallery, he would say: "To begin with we descended into coffee houses like crows from the sky and only later became gradually accepted by the academy."

Gary went to Japan the next year, thus missing the flourishing years of the Beats. He even denies that he was a member, though when he returned from Japan years later, he did bring spiritual sustenance to the already beaten generation.

❖

Gary's life has a storybook quality to it. After spending a year in college he went to sea, and then after coming back to land, he worked as a forest ranger in the mountains of the Pacific Northwest. At Berkeley he studied East Asian languages and translated the poems of Cold Mountain, and then like Cold Mountain before him, he departed for Japan. Gary stayed in Japan for a dozen or so years, three of which were spent as a Buddhist monk. Finally, after his master's death, he returned to the ordinary world, thus bringing American poetry a new note and the environmental movement an important spokesperson.

When I ran into Allen and him for the first time in Beijing in 1983, he showed me a photo of the California mountain cabin that he and his friends had built with their own hands. Our meeting that time was done in secret and, probably owing to my paranoia, I came away with the misperception that both the house in the photo and the people around it were all a bit off kilter.

Ever since last spring I have been planning to go to the mountains and pay homage to his "temple," and to find out exactly how they all began to "go mad." But events have conspired against me, and I have not yet been able to go, as Gary's wife was diagnosed with cancer, and it would be bad to disturb them. According to Gary, aside from having a Zen meditation hall, his "temple" is pretty much like any other American farmhouse. He doesn't reject modern technology: the place has a stove, television, telephone, fax machine, and a modem, but their toilet facilities are primitive.

He told me a story about a couple who came to visit. The wife, having come from the *civilized* world, rushed out of the outhouse, shouting in terror: "There are spiders in there!" Her body had been completely unable to function in the setting, and she asked Carole where the nearest facilities with running water were. Carole told her that they were twelve miles away in a gas station. So, the couple drove the twenty-four mile round-trip to use a civilized toilet.

I have no idea how he was talked into it, but Allen also bought a piece of land near Gary's place. The poet who had been driven mad by modern civilization found it utterly impossible to move away from the civilized world, as it only made his malady worse. Allen had talked about this piece of land to me, saying he would eventually build a house on it and have friends over.

Allen always tried to tell Gary's story in his own way, a considerable investment for him, or at least an investment in friendship. When we were in Seoul, Allen told me how he had sat in meditation with Gary, and whenever he brought him up, he showed a respect that he rarely accorded anyone else. Allen's belief in Lamaism had clearly been partly inspired by Gary, but with the inevitable modification — Lamaism is a bit "wilder" than Buddhism. Gary's belief in Buddhism is intellectual and experiential, in that he focuses on its essence rather than on external observance; takes in the faith in its full diversity without going to extremes.

He told me that he was taken with Marxism in his youth and still thinks that some of it makes sense. I asked him if he ever had a mind to fuse Marxism and Buddhism. "No," he said decisively, "Buddhism contains vastly more wisdom than Marxism." He then went on to say that "the vanguard" is one of the key tenets of Marxism, but that it is an idea that has transformed itself. In the beginning, "the vanguard" referred to the working class; when the idea arrived in China it referred to the peasants, as their support was needed in order to take power; by the 1960s it referred to students and their capacity to rebel; finally French thinkers were unable to cope with their solitude and declared that "the vanguard" was themselves.

Gary teaches only one semester a year in the English department at Davis, and always the spring semester. He drives in every Tuesday and stays in a motel for three nights. Aside from teaching, taking part in departmental meetings and arranging poetry readings for the school, there seems to be a constant stream of friends, colleagues, students, disciples, poetry-lovers and reporters waiting in line to see him. Busy as he is, we are still able to find time occasionally to have a meal together. But the time for this meal always has to be squeezed from the closely packed space in his tiny appointment book. We usually go to a French restaurant, Soga's, which sounded at first like a term of Japanese abuse. It is tastefully laid out and the clientele comports itself like French aristocracy; speaking in low tones at all times.

Gary has the ability to put people instantly at ease. His eyes and voice seem to be urging you to follow him to a place beyond human vexation. In Gary's view, people still have not really discovered America. They are a gang of invading bandits who have occupied the space but don't understand it; they don't know where they are.

Faced with the American mainstream, he continues to advocate a counter culture opposed to monopolization and supportive of cultural exchange; and a return to nature. He believes that this counter culture should base itself on forty thousand years of human history, and that today's rotting civilization remains a pathological illusion.

We agree that I will drive up into the mountains to visit as soon as Carole gets better. It is a vague promise, but one that each of us holds dear. It is a promise that has lasted for forty thousand years.

The Knight-Errant from New York

Eliot is a skeptic. Even when he says nothing, his eyes, expressions, and gestures are all capable of raising doubts about anything around him. This is not surprising, as he is a prototypical New Yorker, and New York has long since taken its leave of the United States. Everything else aside, the roar of the place is completely distinct; the blaring of sirens day and night drives outsiders crazy. A New Yorker has to have extraordinary perseverance and the capacity for doubt in order to survive. Eliot was born in New York and grew up in New York.

He and his wife Nina were born in the same hospital, not, of course, at the same time, and it was not until much later that they met. But I still believe it was New York that introduced them — *You're a New Yorker? Yes, and you? Of course.* Eliot could not live anywhere else in the United States.

In Greenwich Village, the sparse trees on the nearby, rather tranquil West Twelfth Street play an important role, as they are the only register of the changing seasons. The red brick buildings are delineated by rusting fire escapes and their shadows are poorly drawn sketches. This type of row house, also common in England and Holland, embodies a kind of bourgeois mentality.

When one enters the front door there is a living room and kitchen, and outside the kitchen door a courtyard-like backyard. A narrow staircase leads to the children's bedrooms and up another level is the master bedroom. Finally one reaches a spacious loft, its four walls lined with books, and above that a skylight that opens onto New York's dirty sky. Eliot, the owner of the study, is smoking a cigarette and the smoke ascends along with his meditations. I like his cigarettes. They are like small cigars, but very mild. After I gave up smoking there were times when I could not resist their lure.

Eliot has often urged me to move to New York, like a preacher urging his flock to move to heaven. Beyond informing me of its many advantages, he makes a special point of telling me how safe it actually is, and that anyone who thinks otherwise has simply been deceived by Hollywood. He insisted upon this right up until the evening that a thief lowered himself through the skylight and stole his fax machine. This shut him up. If he had been there at the time, meditating with cigarette in hand, the real damage would have been psychological — his inspiration would have been the thing stolen.

I first met Eliot in 1988, at a reading of Chinese poetry organized by Ginsberg in New York. We barely said hello to one another, but my first impression was of a sensitive if melancholy person. I next saw him a year later at an American PEN meeting. That year was a turning point for me and for many other Chinese. Eliot invited me, along with several other Chinese writers, to a discussion on Chinese culture that he was organizing. The audience was quite large that day, and included Octavio Paz and his wife, who happened to be in New York. Eliot had been Paz's English translator from the time he was nineteen, and after meeting the Paz's, Eliot, Duo Duo and I, along with the simultaneous interpreter for the meeting, Iona Man-Cheong, all went out to dinner. With a poet as prominent as Paz in our midst, the conversation naturally gravitated to South American poetry and politics. With the flickering candlelight reflecting in his glasses, Eliot said little, smoking cigarettes and occasionally laughing. He has a strange laugh; short and a bit throaty. He had been Iona's classmate in London, studying Chinese. He used his Chinese, on that evening, to say enigmatically: "I can't speak Chinese."

Eliot and I were born in the same year, but he is six months older. I have suggested to him that, since we are the same age, we should write a book together that would record our experiences in chronological order. We have many things in common. For instance, neither of us completed our educations. When I was serving as a Red Guard, he was a hippie who studied at Yale for only a year before heading off to make his own revolution. He never went back to college, instead wandering hither and thither on "the mighty east wind." He is a moderate among American radicals, and would qualify, according to our standards, for the "carefree faction."

In 1994, we gave a reading at SUNY Stony brook. He had wandered here twenty-seven years before, temporarily taking a friend's place as an editor at a student newspaper. Returning to his old stomping grounds, he was extremely moved and surprised to run across one of the sites of his youth. As we walked by the library his face suddenly lit up. Back then, when a group of radicals were preparing to burn down the library, Eliot had stepped forward and explained the importance of books to the hotheaded students, ultimately managing to stifle their rage.

It is difficult now to imagine the cynical Eliot being so indignant and emotionally wrought up as to give such an impassioned speech. Just when he was defending the SUNY library, my friends and I were sneaking into a shuttered Beijing library to steal books. Different actions; same motivation.

Perhaps resulting from his memories of that possible fire, he has an instinctive wariness of revolution. Two years ago at a meeting on the topic of poetry and revolution, a famous Afro-American poet delivered an address in which he looked forward to the brand-new world to be brought about via the flames of revolution. Eliot coolly retorted that the flames of revolution would only incinerate poets, destroy any sense of conscience, and create a series of bloody tragedies. He cited Russia and China as examples. Eliot was attacked for this from many quarters. In general, while there is a multitude of factions among American poets, they mostly keep to themselves, rarely developing the sort of poisonous addiction to personal attack so common on the Chinese literary scene. Eliot was not so lucky this time, something undoubtedly related to his skeptical attitude and coldly ironic disposition.

Four years ago he edited an anthology of anti-academic American contemporary poetry, which many poets took as a significant event in American letters. But an erstwhile friend fell out with him over this, attacking him as a "racist" and "imperialist," and going on to accuse him of being narrow-minded and intent upon destroying the American poetic tradition. This caused Eliot, who had just given up cigarettes, to fume smoke from every pore. He called me on the phone: "Racist? That's the worst fucking thing you can say here; you can be taken to court for it . . . ."

Eliot and I also share the same publisher. Whenever I go to New York, Ms. Fox, our editor, takes the two of us out to lunch. In New York this must be considered hard to come by leisure time. We generally sit in the window, from where we can see the passersby scurrying along.

In the glitter of glasses and clinking of flatware, I notice a few things that never seem to change about New York: we are here at the same hour and at the same restaurant, with the same desserts and the same topics of conversation. After lunch, Eliot always asks me over. His house is only a few blocks from the publisher. The radius of his activities is about a mile across, and within the scope of this: he buys his papers, visits friends, goes out to eat, and lives life with Nina, his wife, and their two children.

Not long ago Eliot and I attended a poetry festival in Hong Kong. One day a friend took us on his boat out to sea far from the city and we dropped anchor at a small island in the area, after which we went to a white sandy beach by sampan. It was a beautiful day and Eliot and I walked barefoot on the beach, picking up seashells. He suddenly blurted out: "A good father cannot be a good writer, and a good writer cannot be a good father." He provided several examples, the first of which was Octavio Paz.

Eliot felt that he himself loved his kids too much ever to become a great writer. I tried to refute him, since there are numerous counter-examples, but I couldn't think of any at the moment. I realized that in the deepest part of his mind this anxiety had been festering all along, an anxiety no doubt common to many writers. In fact, there are a number of homologies between written work and children and writers and fathers, divisions that just happen to reside on either side of the border between literature and life — fathers and children on one side, writers and their work on the other. And if they are ever conflated, such as putting children together with authors, or fathers with literary work, a certain amount of tension inevitably results.

Yesterday I told Eliot on the phone that I was writing about him. He warned me: "Don't say anything bad. I have friends who understand Chinese, you know." Although we have known each other for many years, he remains a bit of a mystery to me. He rarely talks about himself. But in the end, how much can one person really understand another's life — that most baffling of things? At times I think he resembles a medieval knight-errant-nostalgic — suspicious, loyal, disdainful on the surface, but possessed by a hidden inner impulse to complete some sort of errand.

Eliot is a New Yorker born into a Jewish family who made it through his first year of college. He writes, translates, and edits. He does not believe in any religion, loves his family, and opposes revolution.

CLAYTON AND CARYL

We drain our glasses. Clayton's bathrobe is half open, revealing the gray hair on his chest. "You guys can eat and drink and have a good time while I slave away — I have to teach tonight," he says with a smile. We have known each other for three years, but it is as if we have been friends our entire lives. Our initial relationship as colleagues quickly turned into friendship, and later it was as if we were family. Clayton turned sixty-two this year. Fourteen years my senior, he could be considered my "American uncle." They were upset when I moved to California, and still tell their friends: "Bei Dao abandoned us for the California sunshine."

Clayton is a poet. At one point if you admitted to being a poet in the United States, other people would keep their distance, sensing poverty and mental disorder. Now, however, the situation has changed somewhat. Beginning in the 1970s, the addition of creative writing courses to American universities was a huge net that brought to shore schools of roving poets. One of these "fish" is Clayton Eshleman — a professor of poetry at Eastern Michigan University since 1986. There are some people who condemn the system, thinking it will ruin American literature. "Nonsense!" says Clayton as his eyes widen, "The people who indulge in this sort of derision all seem to have their own trust funds. If it weren't for creative writing classes, I'd be driving a fucking truck in LA."

Clayton was born into an ordinary household in Indiana. His father worked in the slaughterhouse and his mother was a housewife; their lives had no contact with literature. He remembers one birthday when his mother asked what kind of gift he wanted. He thought for a moment, and then said that he wanted a book of poetry. His mother was amazed, but nonetheless honored his request and gave him a book that she herself did not understand. He still recalls the look of perplexity on his mother's face as she handed him the anthology.

Harboring this yearning for poetry, he left his mother and went to college where he wrote poems, translated, published a magazine, taught, and took part in the anti-Vietnam war movement. Still harboring this yearning for poetry, he left the United

States and drifted to the ends of the earth — Mexico, Japan, France, and Peru. His trip to Peru was part of his work on translating Vallejo's "Poemas humanos," which eventually became part of the *Complete Posthumous Poetry* of Vallejo's work, for which Clayton received the National Book Award in 1979.

Clayton does not have the best of tempers, and while he has made many friends, his enemies are also numerous. For over fifteen years he has put his soul into his journal ("Caterpillar," later metamorphosing into "Sulfur") which has resulted in it becoming one of the country's most important venues for poetry. He always says exactly what he thinks. He will, for instance, urge you in a rejection letter to find a different line of work; something tantamount to urging someone who had considered himself the world's finest poet to commit suicide.

When Clayton was young he looked like Jimmy Carter. In the late 1970s, he, Caryl, and a Czech friend were having dinner in a Prague restaurant. When the bill came, it was considerably more than they had anticipated, as the price of the fish had been based on a rate per hundred grams. They began to argue with the manager, at which point Clayton announced: "How dare you take advantage of Jimmy Carter's nephew — we'll see what comes of this!" The manager blanched in terror and profusely apologized, bringing out the VIP register. As Clayton signed it, their Czech friend turned deathly pale.

❧

Caryl is an authentic New Yorker, having grown up in a working class section of Brooklyn. Her youthful craziness was a fact I inferred from isolated bits of their conversation. She eventually left home to live in Manhattan where she indulged in the lovable "ultra-leftist infantilism" of the 1960s. Caryl is still quite attractive, and it takes only a glance to tell that she had been a real beauty. She studied art, worked as an art director at an ad agency, and designed jewelry; she now assists Clayton in publishing his magazine.

Caryl is intelligent, sensitive, and with ideas all her own, but putting this down in so many words simply do not do her justice. She is a distinctive person, in that it seems as if she does nothing — or rather that she does not need to do anything — while she is extremely particular about everything, whether it be poetry or food.

Caryl's life is limited to the indoors, as whenever she steps outside there is always some kind of trouble. If she doesn't sprain an ankle, she will trip and break a finger. Last fall, Caryl and I took my daughter out for ice cream. We had just crossed the lawn when Caryl was stung by a large wasp. That was a warning, and I believe that from then on Caryl has redoubled her determination never to set foot outside the house.

They are a match made in heaven; they were both in failed marriages before this one. Caryl told me that Clayton made a strong impression on her when she first saw him at a banquet.

He was carrying a dripping piece of rare roast lamb across a snowy-white carpet. As far as I can tell, this image is purely aesthetic, as if Clayton had written down a poem for her on a piece of white paper.

Good food and fine wine are essential to the enjoyment of life. They once invited me to dinner at a first-class restaurant in New York where they ordered caviar and champagne. The three of us spent almost four hundred dollars, a sum I almost choked on, used to simple food as I was. Whenever it is my turn to pay, they are just as heedless, and I sit in terror as they order. Needless to say, a professor's salary cannot continually support this kind of expense, so they have set up their own kitchen where they have mastered the art of cooking; they are proficient at any style and region.

Everything was strange when I first got to the States, so I often ended up as their guest. When evening came, Caryl turned on the lights, Clayton put on a white apron, and they busied themselves in their fully equipped kitchen. Their preparations were as complex as Chinese cooking, and it was under their influence that my Chinese stomach finally became able to appreciate other culinary cultures. Sometimes I would even call ahead and tell them what I wanted to eat, to which they would reply abruptly: "We're not a restaurant, there's no menu here."

There is a science to drinking wine. Things like the vintage, place of origin, and vinter's name can all be learned from books, but developing a discriminating palate takes experience and understanding. I once accompanied them on a trip to the Napa valley for a wine tasting. With expressions of the purest sincerity, they listened as the experts at the winery used complicated technical language to describe the color, flavor, and feeling of the wine. During this discourse, they held the wine in their mouths, swirled it around for some time as if chanting Buddhist sutras, and then spat it out. I tried to imitate them, except that I swallowed everything, and before I had tasted many different varieties, the room began to spin.

Whenever friends come over Clayton opens bottle after bottle. And the more he drinks the more he talks, and the talk always becomes increasingly wild until he ends up speaking entirely in physical gestures. He puts on his beloved jazz and moves about, casting a huge shadow on the wall — another night of unrest. On the drive home after visiting other friends, Clayton invariably pronounces orations full of philosophical implications on the topic of our dependence upon the land for our very lives, an oration each time interrupted by the sound of my snores.

Clayton and I often played language games after we had a drink or two. Since my English was poor, I often mistook his meanings with unpredictable consequences. We jumped from word to word, with one implication mutating into another.

Once I asked him for help in choosing a name for an anthology of English translations from our journal, and he immediately tossed out a line from Pound's first Canto: "Ill fate and abundant wine." But I heard "abundant" as "abandoned," which I went with, and as a result the book became *Abandoned Wine*.

When the anthology came out I sent him a copy; Caryl liked the title but he did not. One way or the other, however, it is metaphoric, and in the real world we all agree that wine should never be abandoned. And we drain our glasses.

MICHAEL THE STRANGER

I had just received a postcard from Prague: "Singer says that life is a dance on your grave. Let's meet. Your American Uncle, Michael." The postcard bore a nostalgic black and white photo: a coffee cup and a wild chrysanthemum with the words "Globe Bookstore and Coffee House." It was Michael's characteristic style.

He was probably sitting in that English bookstore in Prague even now, sipping coffee in a melancholic black and white mood, waiting for his gorgeous lover.

49

Michael and I met at the 1985 Rotterdam poetry festival. It was the first time I had been out of China, and I was dizzy from the changes in cultural and linguistic zones. Michael's sad eyes made me remember what he had said; that he wanted me to come to London next year to give a reading. I duly showed up in London at the appointed time and read at a small theater in Covent Garden. A woman poet from Romania was on the same program, but at the last minute her government had refused her permission to leave. Michael stood under the spotlight and chose his words carefully as he obliquely criticized the Ceaucescu government, not wanting to get the poet into any more trouble. After the reading, Michael took me to a bar where he introduced some of his fellow poets. Only later did I learn that in order to put together the sum of money needed to bring me to England, Michael had to act like the protagonist of a Kafka novel, knocking on door after door of numerous bureaucratic offices.

Michael is three years older. He moved to London from the United States in the early 1970s, settled down, married, and took on a London accent. Why had he left America? In an interview he once responded to reporters: in search of the spiritual home of poetry, like Pound and Eliot before him. The British empire, however, did not pay any attention to this solitary American knight-errant.

He invited me home. Their standard of living was poor by English standards, but they still managed to maintain a scholarly dignity: books were the most prominent feature of the house. He worked half-day at the local public library and managed to support, with some difficulty, a family of four. His wife, Hannah, was Polish and was clever and able. His younger son had just been born, while the elder, Gabe, was four or five, and much more serious than most children his age. I thought this little Michael provided a more or less accurate reflection of his father's difficult circumstances: forcing his boring life as a petty official to protect his poetic world. When we discussed poetry, his eyes moistened, and his language became more incisive; there was no doubt that this was the Michael who had originally come to London to make his mark on the world.

I seemed to have a destiny with England, as the same Great Britain-China Centre that had provided assistance for this event was also inviting me to spend a year at Durham University as a visiting scholar. In the spring of 1987, my wife and I took our two-year old daughter to this quiet university town in the north of England. I buried my head in my books, only occasionally looking up and catching sight of its famous cathedral.

Every time I visited London, I dropped in to see Michael. Out of my sense of Chinese manners, I invited Michael to visit Durham when he found the time. I didn't really expect that Michael would set out with his entire family, and I was in a bit of a panic when they showed up. We were even poorer than they were, and we didn't even have a presentable bed for them to sleep on. Fortunately the poor are not picky and they

slept on the floor. Temporarily leaving London and his posi-
tion as a librarian, Michael was transformed into a charming
dreamer. He had all sorts of poetic plans, which he related
effusively to me, his audience of one. And when my wife, Shao
Fei, was in between making meals, he dragged her into his
fantasies. He insisted that Shao Fei illustrate his first book of
poetry, the birth of which an Irish publisher was respectfully
awaiting. His giddy hopes for poetry interwove themselves with
the children's wailing. When Michael and his family departed
one morning three days later, I was unable to return to my
reading; all I could do was sit and stare at the cathedral.

When we left England we visited the United States, after
which we returned to China. My post-June Fourth wander-
ings followed and I lost contact with Michael. In 1990, I went
to England to give a reading, and while I was in London I gave
Michael a call. Michael was momentarily taken aback, then
said in surprise: "My child, where are you? I've been looking
for you!" For a homeless exile calling from a curbside tele-
phone booth, these words were almost too much to bear, and
I couldn't hold back my tears. We arranged to meet in a restau-
rant, to which Michael once again brought his entire family.
After we sat down, Michael scrutinized me from behind his
glasses with his intelligent, melancholic and thoroughly blood-
shot eyes. He had obviously put on weight and it seemed as if
age and the pressures of family life were conspiring to force
him to conform. There was definitely now another Michael

talking. He had grown to detest the world and its ways, and had nothing but abuse for the decadence and snobbery of the British poetic realm; I was shocked to hear him talk this way. I asked about the book of poetry that Shao Fei had illustrated, which made him even angrier: the publisher had canceled his contract. It looked as if the world was intent upon destroying this poet. After we two despairing brothers had spilled our resentments of the world, everything fell suddenly quiet as we drained the remnants of our glasses. I looked over at his sons and suggested going out to buy a couple of books for them.

When we went into a neighboring bookshop, Michael's expression suddenly brightened, as if an internal lamp had been lit. He chose a book for each of his sons and had me inscribe them. He enjoined Gabe to take good care of his book, as if it were not merely a book but a spiritual testament. Gabe raised his head and looked first at this father, then at me, and said quietly: Thank you.

We didn't see each other again for a number of years. I received postcards from Michael from time to time, but they were all brief and disjointed, like notes for a poem. His writing was so small that it almost vanished on the page. I made a request that he use a typewriter, to which he grudgingly assented. He rendered his anger and despair poetic — his poems got better and better, with each word carrying real weight.

I unexpectedly received a phone call from him in 1993 while I was in Holland. He told me enthusiastically that one should love life, after which he said that he was no longer trapped in the library, but was now manager of the Prague book festival, run by a company in London that paid him a decent salary. That is to say, he had joined the real world. I was genuinely happy for him and thought that perhaps this move would enable him to breathe freely outside an all consuming bureaucracy; at least he could use his "free phone" to call me and chat. After I moved to the United States he woke me up each day with a phone call from London. His conversation jumped from point to point: aside from poetry he began to complain about his work, his boss and his fellow employees, then he began complaining about his wife. Hannah had become a virtual monster, wanting to control what he said and wrote. I could sense a family tragedy in the making.

In the spring of 1995, Michael insisted upon my participation in the International Writers Festival in Prague, but he couldn't come up with any money. So, for the first time in my life, I paid my own way to a reading. It was clear to me how much Michael loved Prague. He took me out to the discos every night, but they were much too noisy for me. In the midst of the palpitating rhythms Michael revealed to me that he had had an affair with a Czech girl while he was in London. His eyes grew moist. He also told me that the Czechs had canceled the rights of his company to run the international book festival, and that all that was left for them to do was to put on fashion shows. I tried to comfort him: at least he would be with attractive women all day.

In summer of the same year, I took the train from Paris through the channel tunnel to London for Michael's birthday dinner. I brought along a fashionable tie and a bottle of red Bordeaux, and went with Hu Dong, a poet living in London. Michael had already separated from his wife and the two of them were waiting to file for divorce. He had rented a nice apartment in a wealthy suburb in north London. It overlooked a pond in which the evening clouds reflected.

There was no one living with him — Michael alone. We opened the wine for a birthday toast. After a few drinks he became more voluble and began complaining about how Hannah had used the divorce proceedings to take Gabe from him, and how she was now preparing to extort money. Before we left for the restaurant, he called Gabe on the phone and told him that I was visiting, causing me to recall my role as executor of his spiritual testament.

Michael lost his job and decided to move to Prague. His journey that had begun in the United States had passed through London and ended up in the center of Europe, some twenty-five years after he set forth. The speed of his journey was woefully slower than the speed with which transnational capital was able to nullify his dreams; Prague was becoming increasingly commercialized and he was once again a few steps behind. Moreover, what was to be done about Gabe?

Two years ago around the New Year, I sat under a beach umbrella in Miami drinking beer with Michael. His aged step-father lived nearby. This was the first time we had ever met in the United States, and I blurted out: "Don't you ever want to come back to the States?"

"No, this is not my home any more. I no longer have a home, just like you." He laughed.

GOD'S CHINESE SON

The plane began to descend. From the window I could make out the Salt Lake and large areas of land along the shoreline cut up into different colored chunks. The plane's shadow skimmed over the ground, as if it would not quite come into focus. In the back of the cabin there were people singing hymns, while the other passengers and I pondered the strangeness of it all — we were landing in the sacred realm of Mormonism, Salt Lake City.

The hotel faced a mountain, and outside the window numerous insects had gathered, preparing to hibernate. I pulled out the English draft of my talk and recited it to the bugs.

At the University of Utah, the Lanner Lectures are held once a year. The speaker this year was Jonathan Spence; I was purely an accessory, brought in as a commentator. I received the text of his lecture just before leaving, threw together my response, and faxed it to a friend who then translated it into English. All that remained now was to deliver it cleanly.

Spence's Chinese name is Shi Jingqian. As an Englishman abroad, he has never been willing to take American citizenship, stating: "Why should I betray Shakespeare?" The truth be told, I have a bit of a bias against historians. They all seem to be a little bit too much like workers at the auto yard; classifying the parts of demised cars, and then sitting and waiting for drivers in search of company and a bargain. Jonathan Spence, however, disdains this company and is more concerned with individual lives within history, lives for whom he expresses the deepest sympathy.

Most of the works are biography. This includes his account of the emotional progress of a sovereign in his monograph on the Kangxi emperor, the amazing stories of a missionary in *The Memory Palace of Matteo Ricci*, the unfortunate life of an ordinary country woman in *The Death of Woman Wang*, and the vicissitudes of a mission doorkeeper who happened to end up in Europe in *The Question of Hu*.

It seems to me that it would be more appropriate to say that he is a writer rather than an historian. Moreover, since history is basically made up of stories, it all depends upon your methods of analyzing it.

Tonight was the reading. I had run into Spence and his wife, Chin Ann-ping, in the hotel lobby just after they had arrived. Spence looks a great deal like Sean Connery, and Ann-ping told me that he is, in fact, often stopped on the street by strangers asking for his autograph or to be photographed together. I wonder if Connery has had similar experiences — "Aren't you Jonathan Spence?"

In the spring of 1991, I accepted an invitation from Oxfam to go to Boston to take part in a fund-raising reading for African refugees. They invited Spence to read the English translations of my poems. The evening before the recitation, Spence's student, Iona Man-Cheong, asked us over for dinner. Iona's daughter Harriet was there as well.

Spence arrived with bottles of wine and whiskey. It was the first time we had met. He was resolute, reserved and witty; an English sort of wit. According to Iona, large numbers of female students at Yale had become infatuated with him. That night I was the only one who got drunk, but once I had sobered up a bit, everyone else was still not ready to call it a night, and someone suggested we go see the last showing of *Ju Dou*. After the film, I was still feeling the alcohol and Harvard Square seemed more like the deck of a ship rolling under my feet. The alcohol was still wobbling my brain right up until the next evening's reading at the Sanders Theater. The pained expression on my face was probably misread by the audience as resulting from the bitterness of exile, and was in complete contrast to Spence's graceful bearing and elegant English accent. My pain was also not due to the large numbers of missiles that the American military was launching toward Iraq while we were paying our symbolic respects to the African refugees.

The next year I drove with a friend from New York to Boston, and as we passed through New Haven, we stopped in to see Spence. He was in the midst of a divorce and living in a small apartment in the middle of town. It was one room with four walls: a bed, a table and two chairs, and a small tape recorder. It felt unreal, like the backstage area of a small theater. Our protagonist, Spence, sat there sweating in the intermission between acts. While we ate beef noodles in a small Vietnamese restaurant, Spence told us of his experiences in Guangxi province. He was in the midst of writing a book on the Taiping Rebellion. I could almost see him wearing a straw hat, concealing his nose, and joining the ranks of the peasants as they marched together into his book, *God's Chinese Son*.

New Haven is a dispiriting city; it is filled with homeless who appear to only lack a leader to move them into revolt. Spence led us through streets of outstretched, hopeless hands to a deserted ballet studio, and then into a little room nextdoor, which was his study.

We looked around at the peeling walls and the thick bars on the windows, and could not help commenting: "This really looks like a prison." "Eh?" Spence answered in surprise, "I always thought I was keeping other people out."

The nights in Salt Lake City turned out not to be as desolate as I had imagined; passersby on the streets stirred up the light. After the reading, we went to a private club, The New Yorker, for dinner. A political science professor entangled me in a discussion of Jung Chang's autobiography, *Wild Swan*. He had the extremely peculiar habit of separating his middle finger from his ring finger — that was encased in a huge gold ring, and which looked like a pair of scissors — cutting off my train of thought every time he snipped. At dinner he sat next to Spence, and seemed to want to use his "scissors" to trim Spence's graying sideburns.

The next day we drove to the shrine of skiing, Garden City. After lunch in an Italian restaurant, we strolled through the quiet streets. The sun shone brightly and the snow that had collected on the roofs was melting away.

The couple held hands along the way, just like new lovers. Spence started to talk poetry with me. He and Ann-ping's favorite American poets were Wallace Stevens and Elizabeth Bishop, but they had recently become taken with Robert Frost. Spence sighed and said, "Sometimes I really get sick of history and just want to read more poetry."

In the Spring of 1994, Spence invited Duo Duo and me to Yale to give a reading. He had concluded his intermission and entered the second act. The scene had changed. They had bought a two-story house with Gothic windows in the New Haven suburbs; the garden even had a Chinese pavilion. This was the first time I had met Ann-ping, who taught the history of Chinese religion at a near-by college. Her eyes were constantly narrowed into a smile, as if she were tasting something sweet. Spence was busy attending to the guests, but her every move took hold of his gaze.

We returned to our hotel from Garden City and hurriedly changed our clothes. I am completely incompetent at tying a tie, and ended up struggling with it in front of the mirror like a fisherman who had mistakenly hooked himself. Spence's talk was the final act, and he seemed as unruffled as his tie, but Ann-ping whispered to me that Spence actually gets extremely nervous when delivering lectures, even in the classroom. Under the stage lights his face did seem a bit pale, although he spoke well on the idea of imperial authority in China from the seventeenth century to today.

That evening we went to the hotel bar for a drink. He got a bit emotional when we started talking about his old teacher Fang Chao-ying. When Spence had entered Yale, his advisor, Mary Wright, had told him first to spend a year in the library steeping himself in the literature, and only after that to decide upon a research direction. After spending about a month in the library he became acquainted with Mr. Fang through his reading. He thereupon wrote to Australia, asking if Mr. Fang would accept him as a student. What Spence didn't realize was that Fang was only a librarian, and he responded to Spence's letter by saying that he had never actually directed a graduate student.

Spence was, however, determined, and made a trip to Australia on his own. It was not just Fang's learning that inspired Spence to enter into the study of Chinese history, but also the sort of person that he was. Later on Fang was Ann-ping's teacher as well. As the night drew on Spence took Ann-ping's hand and began to recite a poem by the sixteenth-century poet Pierre de Ronsard. He first delivered the poem in the original French, and then translated each verse into English. It was a poem of love in one's later years.

Very early the next morning I shared a cab with the Spences to the airport. The driver was a tiny old woman. She couldn't open a bottle of Sprite no matter what she tried, and ended up handing it to the back seat, asking "Who is Superman?" I took the cap off for her, and she took a hand-full of pills out of her pocket and put them in her mouth along with the Sprite. "I'm 65 but still think I'm 35. Will you look at that moon! And I forgot to bring this thing along yesterday morning." She grabbed a camera with a telephoto lens and proceeded to take aim at the pale moon as she drove along.

Spence said, "Catching the moon is not easy." The old woman replied, "The key is catching a good moon." The taxi turned a corner and split off from the moon. The woman put down her camera and began to whistle.

JOHN AND ANN

In the spring of 1994, Yanbing Chen and I set out from New York in a car heading north, passing through Connecticut, Massachusetts, New Hampshire and into Maine. The wind swirled snow against our windshield and the occasional roadsign came into view. We went from the interstate onto local roads, then onto a bumpy dirt track. The road signs became more and more irregular, seemingly taking on private meanings. I began to fear that by the time we reached our destination they would turn into obscene, childlike drawings. We came to a dilapidated iron bridge that sang as we crossed it. Yanbing informed me that we would soon be there.

A farmhouse was smoking in the deep woods. We knocked but no one answered. The door was not locked and there were no messages. A kettle hissed on the iron stove, giving off steam that clouded up the windows. We sat for some time, encircled by two flies, until our hosts eventually returned.

John is strongly built and as competent as a forest ranger, though he is a literature professor at Beloit in Wisconsin. He is over fifty and his beard and the hair at his temples have gone white, while the hair on top of his head is still black. I joke that he is freezing from the bottom up.

Ann is much younger than John. She had been John's student. Romances between teachers and students in institutions of higher learning sometimes lead to love, in spite of the regulations against the romance. John was driven out of the Garden of Eden by the authorities, and Ann, as if sporting a red letter, endured the hostile stares for more than a year before she graduated. When she talks about the pressure from that time, she lets out an aggrieved laugh.

We went for a walk before dinner. There was ice and snow everywhere, but the mud had turned soft; spring was underfoot. A stream running into the woods had formed a pond in a depression that attracted a number of wild birds. John and Ann busied themselves clearing away the tree branches that had fallen on the road, and identifying animal tracks. They own nearly one hundred acres of woodland, and we walked for over an hour without ever leaving their property. John told me that recently a number of companies had moved in to buy the land in order to log it. If he and Ann had the money, they would spend it all to extend their property as far as possible. They urged all their friends in the neighborhood to do the same, so as to resist the vicious power that wanted to consume the woods. I imagine that theirs is a pretty hopeless struggle.

They both can manage a few words of Chinese. In '89 Ann was scheduled to teach English at Fudan University in Shanghai. After June Fourth, foreign teachers held heated discussions about whether to go or not. Few others could be persuaded, but Ann nonetheless decided to take the risk. She wanted to be there for her terrified and suffering students during their time of trouble. Not long after, John rushed over from the United States. When their teaching duties permitted, they spent a lot of time with young Shanghai poets, eventually translating an anthology of contemporary Chinese poetry, *Smoking People*. That is when Yanbing met them.

Ann grew up ten miles away in a little town called Mexico. It is a classic blue-collar town that is made up of small, indistinguishable houses. The place reminded me of Chinese society, with cousins, aunts and uncles, and in-laws all living on the same street. A story told here will cross to the other side of town before returning in a wholly different form, but the changes never disrupt the transmission, merely adding to the tale's development. As soon as we got out of the car, the relatives all stuck their heads out, and Ann greeted every one.

When we stepped into the living room, I noticed the smell of dust coming from the furniture, as if it were aging along with Ann's parents. Her father was watching TV and he turned his head to greet Ann and report on the status of her mother's illness. Her mother stuck her head out of the kitchen; her face was flushed but her lips were pallid. She spoke quickly and was not easy to understand. She had been diagnosed with cancer earlier and was now undergoing chemotherapy. She had grown physically frail, and smiled with a sense of her weakness before fate. Ann's father jumped into the conversation from time to time, all the while keeping his eyes fixed on the TV.

This is where Ann had grown up with her six siblings. I could almost hear their hurried footsteps and childish shrieks. Ann took us to the river where we could see the ugly concrete buildings that were the source of her mother's disease. The paper mill had been built at the turn of the century, and had about it the sanguinary odor of all capitalist accumulation. This only source of livelihood for the people of the town was at the very same time a nightmare that tortured them throughout their lives. It was involved in the blood relations of the town, not to mention class, work, in fact all relations among men and women. The pollution it generated drastically increased the incidence of cancer in town. Ann had worked at the factory when she was young; she had both suffered and fallen in love there. Ann is also superb at telling stories, and, during the few days there, we were gripped by the wraiths that emerged from her sorrowful tales. She appeared to have taken an oath to use the white paper produced by the mill to write down segments of its previously submerged history.

Ann's relatives made an exception in accepting John. At first, people had appraised with suspicion this university professor who seduced young women, but John had said nothing, instead using his two hands to demonstrate that he had other abilities. He and Ann used ten years of their lives to turn a decrepit old farmhouse into a comfortable home.

John only sleeps five hours a night. I have had insomnia for many years, and rely on afternoon naps to keep myself charged up. But no matter what time I opened my eyes, John was always there, sitting vigorously at the table with a cup of coffee in his hands, as he had volunteered to copy-edit an enormously thick volume of someone's letters.

One Saturday morning they woke me up, dragged me sleepily to the car, and drove to a local high school where various types of breakfast food were set out on a long table covered with a white cloth. Behind the table were a number of Maine state representatives and senators — the long and the short and the tall — wearing aprons and "serving the people." They poured coffee, put food on plates, and were generally as attentive as they could be. For my part, I couldn't help thinking I should tip them something. To have politicians condescend to this seemed to show the extent to which they will stoop, and I wondered just how many voters would cast their votes in exchange for being served breakfast? A representative came to our table to join us. John introduced us as guests from China, but instead of objecting to the fact that we weren't voters, the politician discussed American policy toward China.

Sometimes Ann teaches English to Asian children in a local primary school. With her optimistic patience, she is perfectly suited to teaching, and it is clear that the children adore her, but what she truly wants is to be a novelist. Obsessed by the paper mill, writing about it is the only thing that can remove the spell it has cast. Her protracted project occupies the only study in the house, where she has come to be the central fixture, a fixed star around which John is forced to orbit. In August, John drives 1,200 miles to go teach at his college, and doesn't get back until December to spend the winter with Ann.

Just thinking about it makes me shudder. Ann will be in this empty house, alone for four full months, writing away while anchored deep in the forest. Even when John gets back for the winter, theirs was still be a world occupied by only the two of them. Maine can get down to thirty or forty below and if a blizzard comes through and snows them in, all they can do is stay at home and pass the long nights in front of the fire. Although I have had similar experiences during my wandering years, my endurance cannot compare. I sense an interior suffering even in their casual conversation, and it is beyond anything I can imagine. Their willingness to put up with it, to not fear it, and to sink roots into the deepest human loneliness leaves me speechless. I express my silent respect for these two lonely souls who give off sparks in all directions.

One night when I was sleeping fitfully, I overheard the two of them fighting. Ann wanted a baby, or at least a dog, and I understood her desire. She cried bitterly in the night, but was laughing again the next day as she told us other people's bitter stories.

John's daughter came to spend the weekend, driving up from Boston with her boyfriend. She is small and delicate; the product of John's love for German literature. In his youth John had translated Rilke, and had brought home from a sojourn in Germany a manuscript of translations and a wife. His daughter had just moved to Boston, found a job, and begun her life there. John's profound pleasure at the visit was evident, but the house was too small, so he insisted that she and her boyfriend sleep outside in a tent. The two young people were quite pleased at the prospect and went out to bed soon after we had eaten. I felt uneasy.

For a young life eventually to take leave of its parents is essentially sad but inevitable, and no one can do anything about it. I tossed and turned in my bed, unable to get to sleep, listening to the gusts of wind. The wind filled the tent outside the house, blowing it away like a sailboat headed out to sea. John's daughter turned over in alarm and tightly embraced her lover.

(FROM LEFT) BEI DAO, DUO DUO, NINA AND ELIOT WEINBERGER, IONA MAN-CHEONG, AND OCTAVIO PAZ AT A PEN SYMPOSIUM IN NEW YORK

Octavio Paz

On the morning of April 17, I parked my car in the overnight lot, took the shuttle to the terminal, and eventually boarded a plane. I hadn't slept well the night before and felt groggy the entire drive down, like a bird dazed by lightening. Getting off the plane, I initially went the wrong way; fortunately there were signs indicating the correct direction. At the shuttle bus stop, passengers moved about slowly, like so many fish schooling by. I got into a van in which the driver greeted everyone who boarded, but without eliciting a single response. He seemed accustomed to this, simply repeating to everyone, "Welcome to Chicago."

It was rush hour, and the road was crowded to the point of being repulsive. At the front desk of the hotel I took my key and a letter that had been left for me and went up to my room with the bellhop. I tipped him, closed the door, and opened the letter: ". . .Unfortunately Eliot Weinberger cannot attend your reading; early this morning Paz died . . . ."

It has been said that the Mexican poet Octavio Paz was the last great master of literary modernism, and that his death marked the end of an era. Despite Paz's literal meaning, he was born in 1914, the year of the start of the Great War, and humanity has not known peace since.

Paz had a large number of paintings and other works of modernist art in his home, which were the fruits of years of friendship and interaction. However, they were all lost in a fire several years ago, a blow from which Paz never recovered. After the fire he lived in an assortment of hotels and hospitals. The Mexican president eventually set aside an official residence for him and sent troops to take care of him, something not altogether different from house arrest. Eliot told me that from that point on Paz became taciturn and uncommunicative, not even wanting to take calls from old friends.

The Chinese American writer Maxine Hong Kingston told me of a similar experience. The Oakland fire of 1991 consumed her house, including her unfinished manuscripts, her letters and photographs; nothing was left. "I have no past" she lamented.

The first time I came across the work of Paz was in the early 1980s, when *Trees are Singing*, an anthology of modern foreign poetry compiled by Wai-lim Yip, was being circulated among our group in Beijing. This anthology was integral to opening our eyes to poetry beyond China. Among them, Paz's "The Street" attracted particular attention: *A long and silent street./I walk in blackness and I stumble and fall/and rise, and I walk blind, my feet/stepping on silent stones and dry leaves./Someone behind me also stepping on stones, leaves:/if I slow down, he slows;/if I run, he runs. I turn: nobody.*

I retranslated it sometime later. What the English version had as "nobody," *Trees* translated "Not a soul," which I rendered as "no one," as it felt more concise and abrupt. The effect of the poem was terrifying to our group, to the extent that whenever we ran into a friend we would joke: "I turn, not a soul," guaranteed to raise hairs on the back of your neck.

In October of 1989, the American PEN Center convened a symposium in New York for Chinese writers with Eliot Weinberger running the show. Much to everyone's surprise, Paz and his wife turned up in the symposium audience. The frenzy of the time was Tianan'men; no one could talk about anything else. When the meeting let out, a group of old friends gathered at the entrance, and it looked as if there was to be another all night session. Eliot asked if we wanted to have dinner with Paz. Duo Duo and I went blank for a moment: would it be Paz or Tianan'men? We of course chose Paz.

We were also joined that evening by Iona Man-Cheong, the interpreter for the symposium. We went to an Italian restaurant where Iona helped me through the menu. Paz had put on weight and looked much older than he did in pictures, but when he laughed he had about him the dignity of old age. We talked about Latin American literature and politics, and Duo Duo asked Paz about his dispute with Borges. "No, there is no such thing, we have always gotten along fine. Perhaps you are thinking of Neruda." And in fact, I did later come across an interview in which Paz expressed his sense that Neruda's Stalinism exceeded political and literary norms.

In October of 1990, Paz received the Nobel Prize for literature. That night he received a telephone call request for an interview from William Tay, representing Taiwan's *United Daily News*. He responded by saying that he had already gone to bed and had just taken a sleeping pill, but this was to be the beginning of his longest sleepless night.

The next time I saw Paz was in December of 1991, at a meeting we both attended in Stockholm. I still remember that the title of the conference was "Serious Literature in Difficult Times." And it certainly was a difficult time for me, as I understood almost none of the proceedings, but still made a brave show of being serious while sitting there. Paz's English was limited and he could scrape by in French. What I remember most clearly was his posture: like an aged lion raising up his head. On the final day, Joseph Brodsky gave a summary report, and in the discussion that ensued, Brodsky's arrogance irritated a number of people in the audience; Paz added a few taunts of his own.

One morning my daughter and I were having breakfast in the hotel dining room. Paz happened to be walking by, saw us, and made a detour over. I ordered a cup of coffee for him. Paz seemed to be in a particularly fine mood, something probably related to the fresh air coming from the harbor, but also perhaps because of a new sense of relaxation — media attention had already turned to the new winner of the Nobel Prize.

To my surprise, he pulled a copy of my recently published volume of poems translated into English, *Old Snow*, out of his bag. He said he liked them, and had been reading them on the plane. He took out a copy of his own just-published collection of essays, *The Other Voice*, signed it, and gave it to me. Unfortunately, I have lost this book in the course of my wanderings.

It was only recently, many years later, that I finally read the Chinese translation of *The Other Voice*, and was dazzled by Paz's erudition and eloquence. He explains the relationship between modernity and literature with great clarity, even as he corrected the serious misinterpretations of the history of "modernism" by Western scholars. Even more important, he embodied his work, *a passion for criticism*, through a highly rigorous theoretical explication.

Li Li, who wrote poetry in Swedish, had arranged for me to meet with a group of young Swedish poets. That afternoon I ran into Paz on a stone bridge in the old city and asked if he wanted to come along, a proposal to which he willingly agreed. Pedestrians were surging by — shoppers, dog walkers, people returning home from work; it was anything but poetic. Paz stood in the weak winter light, his black woolen overcoat thrown over his shoulders, looking like a retired general. When I called him later at his hotel he had changed his mind. "Can't do it, I'm just too tired," his voice was dry and feeble, "You must realize that there are simply too many gatherings like this . . . ." Of course I realized it. The strain of fame over that year had taken years off his life.

Coincidentally, the next stop for both of us was Paris. One evening a week later, Chantal, Gao Xingjian and I were waiting in a Paris hotel lobby when Paz and his wife came down. His wife, Marie-Jose, is French, and at least twenty years younger than her husband. When I suggested going to a Chinese restaurant, Paz was a bit hesitant and entreated me, "Just don't pick any old one. Please choose a nice one." We eventually found a place in the vicinity that didn't disappoint him. We ate hot-pot, drank rice wine, and discussed Tang poetry. Paz had translated the poems of Li Bai, Du Fu and Wang Wei, and had collaborated with Eliot in writing *Nineteen Ways of Looking at Wang Wei*. I drank a bit too much, became sentimental, and began to recite from memory great swatches of the verse of Li Yu, to the anguish of Chantal who was helping me translate. Paz smiled in the candle light.

II

Paz had served as a diplomat for many years in places like France, Japan, Switzerland and India. For poets to serve as diplomats seems like a cultural tradition in Latin America. In protest against the suppression of students in 1968, Paz resigned from his position as ambassador to India, and spent three years in exile in Europe and North America before finally returning home in 1971.

In the spring of 1993, I went to Morelia, Mexico to participate in an international conference on the environment. The conference was meant to be a meeting between scientists and writers. The distinction between wealth and poverty runs like a huge fault line through Mexico. I will never forget the naked children running after the car; such a deep look of hopelessness in their eyes. We investigated a forest in which there was a butterfly breeding ground. Every year millions of butterflies embark from this place through the United States to Canada and then return for the winter — a distance of several thousand miles. Sitting in the forest one can see the butterflies blocking out the sky, their many wings emitting a hum.

I gave Paz a call when we returned to Mexico City and Marie-Jose answered. She called out to Paz in French, and I could hear his response from the other room. He took the phone, asked where I was staying and when would be a convenient time for him to invite me to lunch. Roberto, the young American who worked for Paz's magazine *Vuelta*, accompanied me. Both of his parents are Colombian-American, and he is completely bilingual. I kept asking him why he was not married until I eventually found out that he was living with a gay Cuban writer.

The restaurant was in the hills on the outskirts of the city. From the outside it resembled a monastery hidden in the woods; most of the tables were set up in the garden. Roberto first consulted the list of reservations for lunch, but didn't find Paz's name, and guessed that Paz had probably used a pseudonym. Paz and his wife soon showed up; he was wearing an old hat to ward off the sun, and he had grown a white beard that covered his face like a hairy mask.

There was a guerrilla war going on in the mountains of Mexico's southern borderlands. Conversations swarmed like flies, naturally alighting on this issue's smell of fresh blood. Paz's perspective was the direct opposite of Roberto's. Paz considered it to be the sinister remnants of Maoism, while Roberto argued back that it was a natural response to official oppression. Paz suddenly turned hostile, snapping his fingers and shouting angrily, "What do you Yankees understand? Why don't you all just go home!" Roberto shut up, his face turning a bright red. I immediately changed the subject. Paz was in a particularly bad mood, and soon began arguing with me when I mentioned that I thought W.H. Auden was derivative. Paz snapped back, "If Auden is not original, then who?"

There was a farewell banquet held in Mexico City as part of the closing of the international environmental conference. As the banquet was about to begin, I noticed that the reporters were anxiously awaiting something at the door. High officials and VIPs were unable to attract their attention, but all the flashbulbs went off as soon as Paz appeared. Earlier that day, news reports had broadcast his opinions on the guerrillas, and a number of Mexicans I knew were shaking their heads. I heard from friends that Paz later regretted what he had said.

Because of Paz's celebrity status, he was unable to avoid inspiring envy and anger in others. He was constantly involved in newspaper polemics; debates that were extraordinarily stormy. Eliot told me that a good fight kept Paz young. Sooner or later, however, age lets no one off, and Paz was eventually laid low by illness — first heart surgery in the United States, followed soon thereafter by the discovery of cancer, and then by the insatiable fire that devoured his past.

Only about a month before Paz's death, Eliot had gone to Mexico City to take part in the opening ceremony of the Octavio Paz foundation. Paz attended in a wheel chair and said very little. When people praised his achievements, he merely lifted up his hand, a gesture of fatigue that seemed to say: let this all pass.

March 30, 1994, was Paz's eightieth birthday. Only four years before, his face glowed with health, his step was firm, there was no hint of the shadow of disease or the great fire. The Academy of American Poets held a reading for him at the Metropolitan Museum in New York, inviting such stars as John Ashbery and Mark Strand. For some reason, they added me to the number, which someone told me was at Paz's request. I pulled out a collection of his poetry and inexplicably found myself somewhat disappointed.

From my perspective, his ambition to pursue great narratives had destroyed his secret passion, something that seems particularly clear in "Sun Stone," the very poem that has been declared a modernist classic. Paging back and forth I still ended up choosing "The Street," which maintained the freshness it had when I first read it.

Paz once responded in an interview: "Every minute we become someone else. The person now talking about somebody else differs from the person who was talking about somebody else a minute ago. In this case, who, then, is the other? We are time, and in order to become time we never complete our lives; we are always just on the point of living. Just on the point of living? And what might that be? I have no idea. In the course of asking and responding, we give rise to something that changes us completely, something that changes us into unpredictable creators."

This was probably the first time in the United States that there had been a birthday party on this scale for a foreign poet. The tickets were complimentary; the auditorium at the Met was packed. Not long before the reading began, Paz and Eliot were choosing which poems to read, and Paz suddenly grew flustered, saying to Eliot, "But what should I read? None of them are all that good, really . . . ." Paz became someone else at this moment, someone closer to the Paz I had come to know when reading "The Street": full of doubt, groping in the darkness, stumbling and getting back up again. Eliot eventually calmed him down. At the completion of the reading there was prolonged applause from the audience.

That night I read Paz's "The Street":

A long and silent street.
I walk in blackness and I stumble and fall
and rise, and I walk blind, my feet
stepping on silent stones and dry leaves.
Someone behind me also stepping on stones, leaves:
if I slow down, he slows;
if I run, he runs. I turn: nobody.
Everything dark and doorless.
Turning and turning among these corners
which lead forever to the street
where nobody waits for, nobody follows me,
where I pursue a man who stumbles
and rises and says when he sees me: nobody.

TOMAS TRANSTRÖMER BESIDE BEI DAO IN TOP ROW; JOSEPH BRODSKY (WITH CAMERA) SEATED DIRECTLY IN FRONT OF BEI DAO; MONIKA REACHING INTO THE FRONT ROW ON THE PORCH OF THE BLUE HOUSE

BLUE HOUSE

The Blue House is on a small island near Stockholm; the country home of Tomas Tranströmer. The house is old and small, and depends upon constant renovation and painting to enable it to withstand the grim Swedish winter.

I was in Stockholm attending a meeting at the end of March. The meeting was depressing and pointless, no doubt like similar events the world over. The day before we were to depart, my friend Annika and I arranged to go see Tomas. Stockholm to Vasteras, the city in which Tomas lives, is a two-hour journey. Annika drove a red Saab. The sky was an oppressive shade of gray, with randomly falling snowflakes.

Spring had come late this year, and the gloomy woods were still sunk in sleep; the barren open country undulating along with the highway, dominated by a tone of grayish blue.

Annika had served as a diplomat for some dozen years before unexpectedly becoming a servant of God; a pastor. This had been almost inconceivable to me, as if a long-distance runner had suddenly become a skydiver. And Annika actually does resemble an athlete — tall with short hair, and quite vigorous.

When I met her in Beijing in 1981, she was serving as the cultural attaché in the Swedish embassy. At the time, the West was still an abstract notion of something locked up behind the heavily guarded steel fences of the embassy quarter. Each time I met with Annika, we first arranged a meeting on the phone, and then I waited for her to drive me through the gates. When we drove past the guardhouse, I slid down in my seat like a sack of flour.

At the end of summer in 1983, I went with Annika to the Sichuan restaurant in Yarn Lane at Xidan. As we got out of the car, she gave me a packet of things, saying it was Tomas's new poetry collection, *Barbarian Square*, and included a draft of Göran Malmqvist's English translation and a letter. In the letter Malmqvist asked if I would translate Tomas's poems into Chinese — this was the first time I had heard Tomas's name.

After going home, and with the assistance of the dictionary, I translated nine of the poems. They were formidable. Tomas's images were both strange and brilliant, and in a completely unique register. I felt extremely fortunate to be the first to translate him into Chinese. At that time, China was still at a fairly basic point of departure in regards to Western poetry.

In the spring of 1985, Tomas came to Beijing. I went to meet him at the Bamboo Garden Hotel behind the Drum Tower. The place had been the home of Kang Sheng (the head of the secret police under Mao), and was amazingly large. When we got into the taxi we were both a bit embarrassed. I couldn't get my English working; even gestures combined with spitting out single words didn't work, so I simply remained silent. Over the first stretch of road I remember clearly passing Drum Tower Avenue, going through the rear gate at Beihai, and entering Pingan Lane. We turned again onto Xisi, and continued along Fuwai Avenue heading west . . . but where were we going? There is no way I can now recall; the Toyota cab simply entered a void. All I do remember is my eyes anxiously fixed on the leaping numbers of the meter, as the money in my pocket was very limited.

A couple of days later I was off to the Great Wall with Tomas. The Writers Association produced the car that day and Li Zhiyi, head of the Swedish language group at the People's Pictorial, came along as well. He told the young woman who had been provided as an interpreter by the Writers Association that she could spend the day shopping, and she was only too happy to comply. Li Zhiyi was a great friend, and all we had to do now was to take the necessary precautions against the driver.

In those years we were able to enjoy the advantages of socialism: traveling in an official car to see the sights; dawdling over a free lunch in the Foreign Experts dining room at the base of the Great Wall.

Tomas was very happy that day, his face ruddy with the sunlight that played over its deep wrinkles. He touched the inscriptions left by various visitors on the battlements, and was amazed at the force of people's desire to be remembered. I asked him to look back at me and clicked the shutter. At that moment his arms were criss-crossed and he smiled, the wind lifting up the golden hair that was just beginning to lose its color. This photo would later appear on the fly-leaf of a book that collected a number of translations of his poems, including the ones I had translated into Chinese.

When we were almost to Vastera, Annika called Tomas's wife Monika to confirm the exit from the highway and the exact route to the house. Tomas lived in a dull gray, characterless row-house. I scurried after Annika, who was clutching the address in her hand, looking for Tomas in this maze of modernity. He appeared in the doorway, tossed aside his cane and embraced me.

At that moment I was afraid I would burst into tears. Monika said: "Tomas was about to go out for a walk . . . just take a look at our Tomas, if he hadn't come down with the flu, he would be such a star . . ." I got a chance to take a good look at Tomas only after we were all finally seated. His hair had gone completely white, but his color was good and his eyes had reassumed the look of composure they had had before his stroke.

When I received the news of Tomas's stroke in December of 1990, I immediately called Monika on the phone. She was in tears, "Tomas is such a good person . . . he can't talk . . . what will I do?" Monika is a nurse, and she quit her job when Tomas had his stroke. When I came to visit them in the summer of 1991, Tomas was clearly scared and confused. He was later to describe in a poem the interior darkness he experienced: he felt like a child wrapped in a gunny-sack, looking out at the external world through the thick mesh.

His right side was paralyzed and his ability to speak had been thrown into disorder. He was reduced to mumbling and no one could understand him except Monika. All that existed was Monika standing beside Tomas, looking into his eyes, trying to decipher his inner world. She often guessed wrong, and Tomas had to assist her with gestures. She guessed at time in five-year intervals, and as subtly as tuning a violin, moved her hand right to add, and left to subtract. As Li Shangyin wrote "Hearts in contact will apprehend at once," an idea that came true for Tomas and Monika.

By this time, Tomas was able to speak a few words of simple Swedish, with the word "good" constantly on his lips. Tomas, would you like coffee? — Good. How about a walk? — Good. Would you like to play the piano? — Good. This displayed

the degree of satisfaction that he had in his everyday life with
Monika. I brought a gift along, a CD of Glenn Gould playing
Bach's First, Fifth and Seventh Piano Concertos. Tomas seemed
as happy as a child, all the while winking at Monika. At my
request he played quite professionally a few tunes on the pi-
ano with his left hand. After he finished, he waved his hand
back and forth, complaining that there were too few pieces of
music written for the left hand — so far Monika had "trans-
lated" flawlessly.

The women went in and busied themselves in the kitchen,
leaving Tomas and me to fall into an awkwardness, as if we
were meeting for the first time.

I mumbled a few words, but they were complete non-
sense. I tore off the plastic wrap on the CD and handed the
disk to Tomas. The automatic changer on his player was bro-
ken and tied up with a black string, but Tomas expertly in-
serted the disk. When Gould began playing the first few sec-
onds of the First Concerto, Tomas suddenly burst out hum-
ming the moving first phrase, which startled me.

His eyes shone and then gave way to the great pianist and
the accompanying orchestra, fumbling his way back to his seat.
The music provided an excuse for our silence.

On the end table, the plastic wrap that had been crumpled
into a ball opened slowly like a transparent flower.

II

An oil painting of a multi-masted sailing ship painted by Tomas's father hangs in the Blue House. The house has been there for at least150 years. In order to conserve heat, the ceiling is low and the windows are tiny. If one walks up the creaking staircase, one room is a bedroom and the other is Tomas's little study; outside are the woods. Many of Tomas's images are related to the Blue House.

The first time I saw the Blue House was in the summer of 1985, or half a year after I had accompanied Tomas to the Great Wall. At that time I had been like a mindless fly, bumping up against the glass panes of the bureaucracy time and again, until someone finally waved a hand and let me out.

Tomas was chuckling as he greeted me outside the Blue House. Also there, aside from Malmqvist and his wife (who died last year of cancer), was their student Britta and Annika. Annika had arrived late, having just returned from Beijing to work in the Swedish Ministry of Foreign Affairs. If time were a film, I would rewind and play that episode more slowly, or, better yet, simply freeze the frame. In those days Tomas loved to tease and was as strong as an ox; everyone was well — alive and laughing; Annika seemed as young as a college student, with so much energy that it seemed as if she had just swum all the way back from Beijing.

The clocks stop during the Swedish summer. There is no end to the sun. Sitting outside the Blue House, we drank beer and ate the snacks Annika had made for us; our conversation was desultory. Swedish is similar to Chinese in that it has tones. The sounds of both languages rose and fell, responding to one another as if in a duet. That year the mosquitoes were particularly thick, and looked like a heavy mist when caught in beams of light. Even flailing at them couldn't scatter them. But Tomas sat among the mosquitoes as if they weren't there at all. They didn't attack him and he didn't chase them off. It was as if they had signed a secret peace treaty. Tomas showed me his newly completed poem, "Shanghai" (the title was later changed to "Streets in Shanghai"). The first few lines read:

The white butterfly in the park is read by many/I love that cabbage-white as if it were a fluttering corner of truth/itself

This image came out of his journey to Shanghai. After he left Beijing for Shanghai, he had no one accompanying him, and the embassy told him to save all his receipts. Most of them were written in Chinese,which he couldn't understand no matter which direction he turned them. There are always plenty of people in Shanghai with nothing to do, and they were probably drawn to Tomas's peculiar gestures. The receipts became white butterflies that were read by all of these people.

Tomas used to be a psychologist, and had worked in a juvenile house of corrections. From my perspective, this profession has very close ties with poetry, for isn't poetry, after all, a sort of juvenile offender? At the age of twenty-three, Tomas's first volume of poetry, *Seventeen Poems*, spellbound the Swedish literary world. Even reading them now, they seem all but perfect. He wrote very slowly, and produced only a hundred or so poems his entire life; collected together they would only add up to a small volume. But almost every single poem is great, and that is the marvel.

Let's return to 1998, where we are having an aperitif before dinner. I ask Tomas about his writing, and he takes a notebook of yellow lined paper out of a drawer. December of 1990 is the watershed: before that his letters are clean and precise, but after the stroke he switched to writing with his left hand, and the result looks as chaotic as the aftermath of an earthquake. An American poet told me that as soon as Tomas had concluded his visit to America, someone had slipped a scrap of paper into his room containing a forged verse mimicking Tomas's own hand. When this was "found" again, it was hailed as a great discovery. What would they think if they could see these later drafts?

In the 60s and 70s the Tomas who had refused to adhere to the trends of those times had been ruthlessly attacked by his fellow poets, who accused him of being a "poet for export," "a conservative," and "bourgeois." I remember once asking him whether he had been angered: "I would like to say that I was not, but how could I help it?" But times have changed, and these same people now respect his work, and his numerous literary awards. Monika told me that not long before, the two of them had been at the Stockholm Museum of Art and Tomas had been recognized by a guide, who announced in a loud voice to the spectators: "Our Tomas is here!" and everyone in the museum began to applaud.

At the beginning of 1990, I drifted to Stockholm and ended up living there for eight months. That giddying summer of 1985 had gone and would not return, and I spent every day indoors with the curtains drawn, obsessing over myself. If it had not been for my Swedish friends it is doubtful I could have kept my sanity.

I saw Tomas a lot that year.

There is a photo of Tomas in a flowerbed, dated August 4, 1990. That morning Li Li and I had taken a ferry to the Blue House, but we had missed our stop and ended up on another island. The next ferry wasn't scheduled for several more hours, so Li Li persuaded an old man on the island to take us over in his motorboat. There was nothing we could do to get the old man to take any money from us.

Brodsky was there as well. Since permanently leaving Russia in 1972, he spent a part of almost every summer in Stockholm, it is said, because the climate and surroundings there most resembled St. Petersburg. I didn't like him from the very start, as I was unable to put up with his vigorous sense of self-righteousness, and every time I ran into him after that, my first impression never changed. Brodsky, however, was extremely respectful of Tomas, and admitted quite candidly that a number of his poetic images had been "stolen" from Tomas.

We sat lazily in the sun drinking beer. Everyone was leaning on the railing of the steps up to the Blue House, taking turns photographing one another with a Polaroid. Their daughter Maria, who greatly resembled Monika, helped clean up the glasses. They had two daughters, both of whom lived in Stockholm.

Li Li, Brodsky, and Maria all took the evening ferry back to Stockholm, but I stayed over in a little wooden cabin in the yard beside the Blue House. I couldn't sleep, and an owl called out plaintively the whole night.

In thinking back on it now, there were only four months between then and Tomas's stroke, except that Tomas had predicted his catastrophe in 1974, in his only long poem, "The Baltics." At the beginning of August, I moved from Sweden to Denmark, spending considerable time with Tomas and Monika before leaving. Whenever they came to Stockholm, they gave me a call, and when one is with someone Chinese, a meal is always involved. After a few drinks, Tomas would say, halfjokingly, "I've never seen a Chinese as tall as you before."

In early November I had just settled in at Aarhus in Denmark when Tomas followed me over to give a reading. I sat foolishly in the midst of the audience. Looking back, however, I realize it was a heaven-sent chance to be there just before Tomas lost his powers of speech. His voice was a bit hoarse, but his placid tone seemed to harbor a note of derision that was concealed so well as to be barely perceptible. He emphasized the distance between each word as if crossing a stream by jumping from stone to stone. When the recitation was concluded the audience began to ask questions. A bald man got into a dispute with Tomas. I still felt like a fool, twisting my head back and forth between Swedish and Danish. I had never seen Tomas so agitated, his face red and his voice raised.

The reading over, the host of the event invited us out to dinner. When I asked about the argument, Tomas uttered a single sentence: "That guy considered himself educated." I remembered to ask Tomas for a book of his poetry for my colleague Anna, who had also come to the reading. He stuck his hand into his briefcase and grimaced like a child — none left. None left? I doubted it. None left! He said with finality. A month later he stated that he would never get into another argument.

When I heard the news of his stroke I was devastated. I wrote a poem for him, and according to Monica, he cried:

> *you take the poem's last line and*
> *lock it center heart — it's your center of gravity*
> *center of gravity in a church swinging among tolling bells*
> *dancing with headless angels*
> *you kept your balance . . .*

Seven or eight years had gone by in a flash and Tomas really had kept his balance.

Since I was returning to America in the morning, I had to leave early for Stockholm. We ate dinner. It consisted of caviar, salad and baked fish; there were candles on the table and the silverware sparkled. Tomas's eyes were bright in the candle light. Monika reached out for his hand from time to time, regarding him with an inquiring gaze. After dinner we returned to the living room and turned on the television, as it was time for the news. Politicians approached the camera one after the other.

Monika and Annika started to laugh, but Tomas maintained a very serious expression, his eyes fixed on the television. After a short while, Monica turned off the television and brought out the apple pie she had baked. The three of us began to talk again, but Tomas used the remote control to turn the television back on. Monika explained that Tomas felt responsible for supervising the idiotic politicians.

Monika confirmed that in the summer of 1990 I had, in fact, had insomnia when I stayed at the Blue House. But what had we done the next day? Of course, Tomas and I had gone out to gather mushrooms.

We had worn long rubber boots, looking as clumsy as astronauts. As we walked along it began to rain and the path in the woods became even muddier. Tomas walked ahead, using a pocketknife to dig out the mushrooms. He put them in his mouth to taste, then put the good ones in a bag; the bad ones he quickly spit out, saying *poison*.

PENG GANG

A bit more than a year ago a friend in China wrote seeking confirmation of some news: that Peng Gang had committed suicide. No one knew his whereabouts, only that he had originally come to the United States in 1982 to study at the University of Pittsburgh. We knew that he had completed his Ph.D. in mathematics, but nothing else after that. I was pretty sure that he had, in fact, committed suicide, and I felt bad about it for quite some time.

At the beginning of 1973, after Peng Gang and Mang Ke had spent ten cents on a frozen persimmon, they declared the founding of the "Vanguard Group." Peng Gang's house was separated from the Beijing railroad station by only a single wall. On a whim, the two of them leapt over the wall and jumped onto a train heading south. The night before, Peng Gang had hurt his arm while trying to steal a book from the library. The next day after a major fight with his father, Mang Ke came looking for him; he tore off his bandage and they hit the road. They were thrown off the train twice, at Xinyang and Wuhan, and with their money all spent, they were reduced to selling what belongings they had brought with them. Peng Gang convinced Mang Ke to use their last five cents to clean up and go out looking for a pretty girl to beg from. In the end it was a well-meaning female cadre who made the arrangements for them to return home.

I met Peng Gang that fall. From the back window of Peng Gang's house one could see a gray brick wall. When a train rolled by the window panes rattled in their frames, which, I must admit, was a real enticement. Later on it would be from this point that my own travels would begin.

Peng Gang's paintings amazed me. At the time, based on my limited experience of life, I judged that if this person were not a genius, then he must be insane. In his paintings I could see images of that journey: passengers with cold expressions, fields burning under the bright sun and dilapidated houses along the way. He was generous and allowed me to pick whichever ones I wanted; I rolled up a few and stashed them under my bed after I got home.

Peng Gang was strange looking, somewhat resembling the figures from Picasso's blue period. His most common expression was one of derision, with narrow eyes that always seemed to be taking aim at the world. His speech was just like the shots that follow upon taking aim — fast and accurate. He was exceedingly thin, yet in the winter he wore only a shirt while he rustled through the streets like a shadow. We became close almost immediately — our utterly opposite personalities perfectly complemented one another. I was seeking a type of craziness with a kick like strong liquor, while his craziness was in need of a container.

He gave his diary to me to read. His father had been an engineer who died under political persecution. On the day he received the news of his father's death he wrote: If I had an atomic bomb, I would perish together with the world. Another entry was from two years before when he had attempted suicide. He had swallowed half a bottle of sleeping pills and then used a knife to cut open his thigh. His writing had become a scrawl, but his description was calm and collected: the blood oozes out from the pale wound, white; it doesn't hurt that much . . . it looks like this is all there is to death . . . . The diary breaks off there, when he suddenly decided to live and fought his way to the local hospital to get help. He was only sixteen that year.

If he still had this suicidal impulse some twenty-five years later, one could not help but admire him.

Arriving home one day, my daughter told me that I had gotten a call from a Peng Gang, which alarmed me so much that I called right back. He chuckled into the phone, a sound definitely of this world. Since he spoke mostly in English, he talked about American realities: money, computers and the pressures of work. Don't you know that money is power? He had found me in a phone book in the library. Suicide? Who me? I don't have time for suicide. He didn't live very far away, only two hours by car. See each other? Sure, well, but I've been pretty busy lately . . .

In the old days we saw each other once every few days. He was a master prankster. When we ate in a restaurant he would smoothly scoop the plates and tea pots into his book bag; or, when there was no one around, he would boost an entire watermelon from the grocer. When we went to the outdoor market in a little town in Baiyangdian, he would hustle past each stall, basket in hand, asking prices of the country people at the same time he stuffed his basket full of their fruits and vegetables. He left them totally speechless and amazed.

What year was that? Yes, it was 1974, summer. Six or seven of us had drifted down to Baiyangdian on the train, but had been apprehended as soon as we came out of the station. We announced that we had come to Baiyangdian to engage in rural labor, but the policemen didn't believe us and subjected us to full body searches. Peng Gang was mouthing off, so he got searched the most thoroughly, even having to take off his shoes.

I seemed the most respectable, so the police just did a perfunctory job and let me go. Luckily the money had been hidden on me.

In recalling things past one should never romanticize youth. In those years every one of us was like a lone and angry wolf: suffering, ignorant, selfish and always ready for a fight. There were, of course, good times. I remember that Peng Gang, Mang Ke and I once rowed a boat over to the county seat to get some white potato liquor, the cheapest of the local vodkas. On our way back the wind started up, eventually becoming so strong that it whistled through the tall reeds on the bank, doubling them over. We kept drinking as we took turns struggling to row the boat. The next day we spent the night in the village Dizhuang at the place of our friends who had been sent there to work. We went to the market, where Peng Gang purloined a whole basket of vegetables; enough to make a sumptuous dinner. Inspired by drink, we tuned in some rock and roll on the short-wave radio and Peng Gang and Chen Jiaming got up and started to dance. To see these two scrawny guys twisting and cavorting like snakes made us egg them on even more. When night came, we were still full of energy, so we took the boat back out on the water. The surface was completely flat and the luminous moon filled the sky. Will the parents of this world accept the wanderings of their unfilial sons?

This spring an old friend from that time of my life came to visit. We called Peng Gang. He expressed his astonishment in English on the phone and drove over in a new red Nissan, bringing along some champagne and beer. He had emerged out from under the shadow of Picasso's blue period and was now twice as wide as before. With the added flesh on his face, it was difficult to recall his prior expression of derision. His eyes seemed to be tired of taking aim, but he spoke just as rapidly as he had in the past. His speech was larded with English, and it sprang on about the nightmarish pressures of his work.

He had been very successful in the United States. After earning his Ph.D. at Pittsburgh, he had worked at Harvard and then transferred to Berkeley's famous quantum physics laboratory to do research. Three years before shifting to computer science, he found a good job in Silicon Valley, where he had been steadily promoted. He had not been back to China even once in fifteen years.

Within our circle in Beijing during those years, Peng Gang had been a famous nut. Due even more than to his dissolute lifestyle, this judgment was brought on because of his eccentric style of painting, which ran diametrically opposed to the officially controlled artistic fashion of the time. He did once actually attempt to participate in an official exhibition, with a completely expressionistic work. He painted a female vendor in a food market with a ferociously ugly face. In one hand she was holding a knife, and in the other she was grasping a bloody plucked chicken, with a tub full of freshly slaughtered chickens, ducks, meat and fish beside her. The person in charge of choosing paintings for the exhibition called Peng Gang over, quickly looked him over, and asked: "Did you paint this?" He nodded his head. "Considering that you are young and ignorant, we'll let you off this time, but get the hell out of here!"

He excelled at telling stories, many of which were the retelling of American movies. I can still remember *The Sixth Poplar*, which took him half an hour to tell, including all of the gestures and sound effects. This, combined with the music he added when he felt in the mood, left me in tears. Actually, he hadn't even seen the film, but had heard about it. It was said that the person who had told it to him was even more incredible, and had spent two and a half hours telling the story, which was twenty minutes longer than the original film. When I arrived in the United States I looked everywhere for the movie, but no one had heard of it. Perhaps it was all simply another work in the tradition of Chinese oral literature.

We often went to a small restaurant near my house to drink. One day when we were well into our cups we began to talk about the future, about the prospects for art, and about the end of political despotism. Peng Gang fixed an enthusiastic gaze on me and said softly: "As soon as a movement for liberalization begins in China, we must join up." We drank a toast to freedom.

At the beginning of 1975, our friend Zhao Yifan, who collected underground literature, was arrested. Conditions were tense, so I began to make changes to my letters and working drafts. I said goodbye to my friends and made all the necessary preparations in case I was sent off to jail at any moment. I went to see Peng Gang. He borrowed five dollars from his sister and dragged me to the Western restaurant in the Xinqiao Hotel. He analyzed the situation for me and told me about his experiences from his two periods spent in prison. When we came out, a north wind was howling, whirling the snow. He patted me on the shoulder, said no more, and departed into the gloom. Several months passed by and no policemen came to my door. I began working again.

A split developed between Peng Gang and me in the same way that a bottle and its wine grow weary of one another. One night we had a violent argument as we were leaving the house of a mutual friend. We took the last #22 bus of the evening, perched on the coupling of the joined cars. The movements of the bus jolted us along as the scenery outside the window became a blur. We had hardly been in contact since then.

By the time *Today* began publication at the end of 1978, Peng Gang had already tested into the chemistry department at Beijing University, but he still came around to the editorial offices from time to time. I reminded him that this was the movement for liberalization that we had dreamed of and not to forget the promise we had made to each other. He broke out laughing and said: "Once there was someone who made a vow to every friend he had: if I had a boat, I would certainly take you along. Later he actually got hold of a boat, but it was too small and could only seat two people, and would thus never be able to take along all the people he made his vow to. So, he simply boarded his boat and waved goodbye to everyone." Not long after Peng Gang came to America by himself.

Eighteen years later, I called him to remind him not to forget to write something for *Today*. This time he didn't mention the boat. "My wife just had a baby and on top of my job, I've just started a company. I'm trapped. I even have my own patent. I don't have time to sleep. But that's life, paying the mortgage and trying to scrape together tuition for my son. Maybe later . . ."

THE VISITOR FROM POLAND

The plane had been on the ground for an hour, but there was still no trace of him and I was growing anxious. The new restrictions on immigration that had just been passed by Congress were transmitted via the internet into the brains of immigration officials at all American airports; it was reflected on their frosty faces, rendering them more severe than ever. Liu finally stuck his head out of the automatic door. In the eight years since I had seen him, he had aged considerably, reminding me of his father. He was wearing the same dirt-brown down jacket he had worn in the 1970s, with its soiled collar and frayed sleeves. He seemed to be deliberately mocking Lin Yantong's design for the San Francisco airport, in which travelers are meant to fly into the future.

We got in my car and drove back to the past. He desperately needed a cigarette, which left me no alternative but to roll down the window as wisps of smoke trembled out on the wind. We had known each other for twenty-five years. In the spring of 1972, my high school classmate Tang Xiaofeng mysteriously informed me that his neighbor was the "liaison officer" for the underground artist group "The Vanguard." Both titles held a similar attraction for me. Liu worked as a fitter in a factory, but he was highly cultured, like literati in the old days. Soon after he was released from prison, where he had been for three years for counter-revolutionary speech. Fortunately, he was locked up with a number of prominent cultural figures, from whom he learned a lot listening to all of their stories and combined experiences. He still looked like a prisoner, hunched between his bunk and a little desk, as he told me prison stories that he had sworn to write down. This was how I came to know "the monkey" of "The Vanguard" — the very same person who would later become better known as Mang Ke; and then through "the monkey" I was introduced to Peng Gang. The entire "Vanguard" consisted of these two, plus the liaison officer.

The next day Liu put on an apron, nimbly took up his kitchen implements and made us one of the specialities from his flourishing Chinese restaurant in Poland. In the summer of 1990, he could no longer endure the oppressive atmosphere at home, so he left for Hungary, where he drifted for half a year or so before moving on to Poland. The poet Yi Ping had told me of their strange encounter in Poland. He had asked for directions on the street, which is how he came across the Chinese restaurant. Someone responded to his greeting, opened a basement window and climbed out. Liu's white teeth gleamed out from a face covered with kitchen grime. Liu began by working for his room and board, put some money away, and eventually ended up buying a restaurant in the university district, where he served simultaneously as cook, caterer, buyer, accountant and boss.

Liu's transformation astonished me. In the 1980s he had had the easiest life of all. He was allowed to make a documentary in Tibet for Hong Kong's *China News Agency*, and had a lot of other money on the side with which he bought electrical appliances and Romanian furniture. Actually, it wasn't so much the money as his general attitude: there aren't that many carefree days in life, so you should enjoy them when you can. He often provided the food and wine and invited his friends over.

His speech directly reflected the times in which he lived. At first he spoke at a leisurely pace; when the high tide of commerce came in he began to speak in waves; after June Fourth he started to gasp; finally he gathered his belongings and hit the road.

I am ashamed when I compare myself with Liu. While living abroad, aside from scholarships and teaching my native language to get by, what else can I do? As they say, one must first survive before one can flourish. If intellectuals could grow their own rice and make their own food they wouldn't have to bow and scrape for a living.

Liu's first reaction to America was cautious. He meticulously compared prices — from fresh ginger to automobiles — collected restaurant menus, and paid very close attention to the classified ads in the papers. Eventually I began to see something familiar in his eyes. I had also come from Europe, and I knew the speechlessness of being Chinese in another ancient culture, knew the xenophobia brought on by economic fluctuation, knew also the assorted mirages presented by the new world. Liu wanted to hang on to the American dream, but the response of the INS was: Your dreams can stay, but you have to go.

Liu and I often traveled together in the 1970s. We visited places like Baiyangdian and the Wutai mountains, but at the time we never imagined how far we would eventually go — so far that we couldn't envision home, or were unable to return home, or even that we might not want to return home. In the fall of 1975, I had a fight with my father and left for the Wutai mountains with Liu. The dilapidated temple and the sparse evergreens had a desolate beauty to them as they bathed in the setting sun. We met several monks, most of whom were from farming families and radiated an unpretentious charm. There was also a nun who had been a student in the Chinese department at Beijing University in the 1940s. Why had she departed the ordinary world? There must be some hidden story. In the dim rays of the setting sun the light in the eyes of her wrinkled face shone clearly. We hit it off with her and ended up giving her a book on Buddhist thought written by Ren Jiyu. When we finally ran out of money we jumped a train to Beijing that ran through Datong. As we neared Beijing we began to argue about where we should get off. Liu insisted on getting off at a small station in the distant suburbs, but I was convinced that it would make us too easy a target.

Our faces were bright red with anger as we stared through one another with hostile eyes. We eventually ended up at Beijing Station and managed to get away by jumping over the wall. We then ducked into a bath house at Qianmen, and it was only after a hot soak that we began talking to one another as we relaxed on the benches in the bathhouse, smoking and staring up through the skylight.

But to get back to the story. In those days we dreamt of literature, love, and traveling around the world. Now as we drank together late into the night, the sound of our clinking glasses was the sound of shattering dreams.

Both of Liu's marriages had failed. He ran the restaurant with his present wife only because of the complexities of divorce proceedings in a foreign country. They had postponed getting divorced so often that neither of them had the heart actually to go through with it, so they just let things stay as they were.

Valentine's Day was nearing and my daughter whispered to me: "Why is Uncle Liu buying two valentines?" How could I explain it to her? One was for his wife, motivated by custom and old habit, but the other was for his Polish landlord's daughter, which represented his true feelings. Liu asked me to translate his inscription into English, and to copy it onto the valentine, but he couldn't even spell his beloved's name. I felt very sorry for him: apart from the limited Polish he used at work in the restaurant, how would he be able to express himself? But this, after all, was his only sunlight in the smoke and grime of an alien land.

Liu is mild mannered, erudite and sensible. And according to Yi Ping, completely non-aggressive — something rare indeed in these rather difficult and unreasonable times. His ancestors were farmers in Hebei province, and if it had not been for the revolution, he would have remained a local degree holder, living a peaceful and elegant life.

Then at some point times turned on him, sending him to prison to do hard labor where he almost died behind iron bars. But it was these very experiences in jail that became his fate. After being released from prison he was able to relax for a few days, but soon the political battles started up again and he was forced to depart his native land and follow in the footsteps of

Genghis Khan, working as a cook for his distant relatives. When his mother became gravely ill, his relatives put up all sorts of obstacles, making it impossible for him to return to see her one final time. His mother stared at the doorway until her very last moment.

"I'm trying to emancipate myself now," said Liu as he stuck out one finger after a few drinks. "One hundred thousand! If I can just save one hundred thousand American dollars I can retire and go home." His complexion turned ruddy, sweeping away his prior gloom. Earn money and emancipate himself, go home, back to the countryside, buy a house and some land, read and write a little, and live the life of a country gentleman. This, after all, had been his lifelong dream. From the very first time we had met he was muttering this, but what would the future actually bring?

One day we took a tour boat around San Francisco Bay. The Golden Gate bridge turned over our heads like a gigantic ruler, as if measuring our lives' limits. In honor of our twenty-five years of friendship, we had a photo taken of the two of us under the bridge; twenty-five years is the ruler's smallest unit of measurement.

Two days before Liu arrived, my daughter told me that someone by the name of Peng Gang had called. Could it really be the same Peng Gang of "The Vanguard" from twenty-five years before? It turned out that he had been in the United States for a number of years and had moved to San Jose two years ago. I called him and told him that there was somebody who wanted to talk to him. Liu took the phone and stated his name. Peng Gang couldn't have been more surprised, and he headed out immediately, bringing along champagne and beer. The conversation among the three of us was like mountain climbing — easy when you're young, but clearly much more difficult since we'd all aged. As the sun set in the west, we couldn't help but sigh: our group had all scattered; it seemed that the "liaison officer" had been neglecting his duties.

Liu needed to go back. His restaurant was in dire need of his services, not to mention that his visa was expiring. Just before he left, I accompanied him on a shopping expedition. Everything he bought was related to the restaurant, from things as grand as bamboo steamers to trifles like garlic and ginger, all of which he stuffed into a large cardboard box. When I called to reserve his flight, I discovered that because of a bad connection he would have to wait at the Paris airport for twenty-four hours. I tried to drag him to the French consulate to apply for a transit visa, but he wouldn't go: he wanted to save all his money for his "emancipation." As a consequence, he ran into problems at the airport. The pretty girl behind the counter leafed through his passport as she carefully looked over his cardboard box and 1970s vintage down jacket. She insisted that Liu obtain a French visa. We argued with her fiercely, but it wasn't until she finally called her superior that he was eventually allowed through.

I was distracted for an entire day after he left, but at the de Gaulle airport in Paris, even as the baggage handlers were man-handling his cardboard box, Liu had quietly withdrawn behind a pillar and gone to sleep.

DIRECTOR KING HU

I woke up in a Hong Kong hotel at eight in the morning, and picked up the morning newspaper that had been stuffed under the door. I took it back to bed but didn't see any news of great importance. Flipping through the photos of politicians, whose callousness manifested itself in the effusion of false smiles, I came upon a familiar face. Cigarette in hand, he was talking with an actress in front of a camera — it looked as if his long-planned *Ordeals of the Chinese Laborers* was actually about to begin filming. I looked again at the headline and was shocked:DIRECTOR KING HU DIES SUDDENLY IN TAIPEI.

He had passed away at six o'clock the night before while undergoing a procedure to correct coronary arteriosclerosis at the age of sixty-six. Even if I say that I have seen more than enough death, Hu Jinquan's departure was something that I could not accept. My mood quickly deteriorated and I gave my friend Gu in Los Angeles a call; he had also heard the news. We said little to one another; I was horribly choked up.

I first met King Hu in Los Angeles in 1990. At the time I'd been drifting, so time, place, and people often get fused into a single mass, but I distinctly recall the location, mood, and details of the conversation during that specific meeting.

Mu Xiaocheng, a former professor at the Beijing Institute of Film, and his wife had invited us to a rather elegant Shanghai restaurant, the *Spring Lake Pavilion*. I was utterly ignorant and ill-informed, not only had I never seen any of his films, but I'd never even heard his name. He was not tall, and was getting a bit of a paunch; compared to his body, his head seemed huge, and he had bright, piercing eyes. I was fascinated by his authentic Beijing dialect, a speech unsullied by years of revolutionary upheaval. It inspired in me a memory more remote than simple homesickness.

He left Beijing just when I was born in 1949. He graduated from high school, and at the instigation of some classmates, decided to head for Hong Kong to try his luck. He paid a visit to a relative who was serving as a district officer in the new government to ask for his help. He was sternly reprimanded, but less than two days later his travel pass for Hong Kong was approved. In his essay "Home and Other Places," he wrote: "There was a saying in the 'old society': There are two cities in the world like 'quicksand,' Beijing and Paris; should you happen to live in either place for a few years, you will never want to leave. This saying, however, applies only to outsiders. For people like myself, born and brought up in Beijing, this feeling is nonexistent; in fact, we can't abide the stagnant atmosphere of the place and are always looking for a way out."

He was an avid reader from his childhood, and the first job he found in Hong Kong was as a proofreader at a printer — work that seems to have been somehow preordained. The first thing he proofed was the Hong Kong telephone book, and the second project was even worse: an edition of unpunctuated Buddhist sutras. He took on any sort of work imaginable: doing odd jobs at the U.S.I.S., creating artwork at an advertising agency, working as a set designer at a film studio, acting, and eventually lasting long enough to become a director. He made his name with the film *The Drunken Swordsman*. After that film, he went to Taiwan to film *Dragon Inn*, which did record box office sales for Mandarin movies in Hong Kong. Later he spent three full years making *The Female Swordsman*, which ended up winning the *Grande Prix de Technique Supérieur* at Cannes in 1975.

In 1978, the authoritative British journal, *The International Guide to Film* chose him as one of the five most important international directors, and among Asian directors he received the honor of being ranked behind only Kurosawa. Those were King Hu's greatest days.

He was a perfectionist. When filming *The Female Swordsman*, he wanted to create the bleak scene of an abandoned old house, but he thought the reeds that were growing there were not tall enough, so he opted to wait several months until he could film the reeds at the appropriate height. Being this painstaking in his work, with complete disregard for the budget, he was bound eventually to get into trouble with his employers. He made a number of successive films that lost money, and after that no one asked him to make any more movies.

Over the past decade his only film was *The Lady in the Painting*, which had a great script and important actors, but still failed at the box office. Things were not going well when I met him, which is perhaps why he was so willing to associate with us. Every time I came to Los Angeles for a social gathering, he was there. Listening to Hu talk was a great pleasure. He discoursed tirelessly on the great issues of the day or on matters of no importance whatsoever, but he always riveted us. He not only never seemed to weary of talking, but would never let anyone else break into his conversation. His friends were invariably tactful, and didn't impinge on his enjoyment. And since I am by nature a listener, we got on extremely well.

At the beginning of 1995, I was staying at Gu's house in Los Angeles. The veteran Taiwan journalist Bu Dazhong invited Hu and me out to dinner. I had just gotten up the next morning when Hu called, wanting to have a chat with me first. We talked from 9 a.m. straight through until 1 p.m., then Hu took me to a small Northern-style snack bar for noodles, onion cakes and cold beef. We ate and talked until 2:30, but as I had the habit of taking a nap, I was visibly fading. It seemed as if Hu would keep talking the rest of the afternoon and into that evening's dinner. On the way back to Gu's house I couldn't prevent myself from giving into my old habit.

"You take naps?" Hu seemed surprised and disappointed. And then he added, "You're lucky you can. OK., see you later this evening."

Hong Kong cinematic circles considered King Hu an eccentric genius, which referred to his odd temperament. He made very few films, wrote, exhibited his paintings, and gave lectures. He had collected so many books that he had nowhere to put them all, so he donated a number of them to UCLA. According to his former wife, Chung Ling, his greatest pleasure in life was playing the dilettante. He actually got annoyed when he made a film, because he worked so hard that there was never any time for reading, drinking, or spending time with his friends . . .

What I most admire about King Hu was his universalism and free and easy ability to feel at home wherever he happened to be. He had lived in Beijing, Hong Kong and Taipei, and, like me, eventually ended up wandering to the United States.

125

When people asked him where his hometown was, he would say Hong Kong or Los Angeles, but never mention Beijing.

Last October, Gu and Mu Xiaocheng agreed to drive up from Los Angeles to visit me. When Hu heard about the plan, he eagerly added himself to the trip. Mu Xiaocheng, however, was very busy at the television station where he worked, and they never found a good time to come up. Hu was impatient and tried to get Gu to go with him by Greyhound. For some reason it never worked out, and when I took my parents to visit Los Angeles two months later, Hu had already left for Taipei, missing our last chance to meet.

King Hu died poor and with no children. Various people busied themselves finding a gravesite, having a statue constructed, and creating a memorial foundation. But I still have only one wish — to see a couple of his films.

Gao Ertai, Witness

Some people are difficult to classify. They are invariably eccentric, independent minded, solitary, and either shy or arrogant. In general such people are hard to like. And because they cannot be classified, they are hard to manage and politicians regard them as their natural enemies, whether the politician is a dictator or democratically elected. Gao Ertai is one of these people.

As soon as I arrived in New York I got in touch with him. Gao Ertai is partially deaf, so most of the time the phone is answered by his wife, Pu Xiaoyu. While listening to Xiaoyu's

127

gentle tones, Gao's huge voice suddenly breaks through: "Bei Dao! Welcome," and then disappears. He only uses the transmitter half of the phone, since the receiver is of no use to him.

The first time I met Gao Ertai was at an exhibition of paintings in Chengdu in 1985. Shaking hands with him, I felt the power of his grip and observed how large his hands were. I then noticed his physique: sturdy and agile. He was not comfortable speaking, something quite at odds with his status as a noted aesthetician and professor. As we chatted I caught a glimpse of depression in his eye, when in fact that was probably the easiest time of his life; a break in an otherwise constant storm.

I had heard a story about him. In 1983, while teaching at Lanzhou University during the "anti-spiritual pollution campaign," he had been designated as one of the principal targets of criticism for the whole province. One day the university Party Secretary notified him that the provincial party secretary wanted to speak with him, and sent him a note with the date and time. When the time came, however, Gao was nowhere to be seen, sending the local party secretary on a panicked search all over campus. He didn't find Gao until the next day, and when he did locate him, he was as worked up as a peal of thunder, interrogating Gao as to where he had been hiding. Gao calmly explained that he had not been hiding, but had been in his studio painting all along. The secretary asked him rather sharply why, since he had received the notice, he had not shown up? Gao responded that he had indeed received the notice but that he had never agreed to show up.

Gao Ertai was born in Gaochun in Jiangsu province. In 1957, because he published the essay "On Beauty," he was condemned as a rightist. This oppositional spirit ran through the family, as his father and sister met with the same unhappy fate. Not long thereafter his father fell in the brickyard of the labor camp to which he had been sent and never got up again. In the Gobi Desert labor camp where Gao was sent he was eyewitness to innumerable deaths, and he himself almost starved to death. In 1959, an invisible hand picked him out of the ranks of those waiting to die and assigned him to the Gansu provincial museum to paint propaganda pictures celebrating the tenth anniversary of the People's Republic. He had escaped calamity to be able to bear witness to sufferings that were ten times worse than anything described in *The Gulag Archipelago*. The first day out of the camp he had dinner with the police who had delivered him there; he couldn't even be bothered to chew, just swallowing up vast amounts of meat, and he still has stomach problems to this day as a result.

The next time I saw him was in Los Angeles. In the summer of 1989, he had been sent to prison in Nanjing for six months for "Inciting counter-revolutionary activities." After he got out of jail, he and Xiaoyu escaped overseas through the underground tunnel. The whole arena in which we performed had been turned upside down by a single event, and good

friends and relatives fled to different part of the world, some-
times never to see one another again. I had never expected to
meet Gao Ertai eight years later on the opposite side of the
earth, and I was both surprised and delighted. He had changed
little, but the depression that used to show in his eyes had
vanished and been replaced by a cheerful clarity, like the Cali-
fornia sky. He was hard of hearing, so interacting with him
was difficult.

Everything I said to him was repeated in a much louder
voice by Xiaoyu, a bit like working through an interpreter,
except in this case from Chinese to Chinese. Fortunately, nei-
ther of us regarded conversation as being particularly impor-
tant and we were content to sit together and enjoy the warmth
of each other's presence. Xiaoyu had been Gao's student and
had worked previously as an artist at the Beijing museum. She
had a gentle disposition and seemed quite happy to traipse to
the ends of the earth with her former teacher.

They had supported themselves in those years by making
paintings for the Hsi-lai temple in southern California and
had lived a simple and fulfilling life. When we took our leave,
I was so moved that I wanted to embrace his sturdy shoulders.
This desire came not out of pity, but out of pride.

As I later read the continuing installments of his mem-
oirs, *In Search of Home*, I would recall that instance of pride.
China is not short of suffering, but is short of art about that
suffering. Gao Ertai's stories take us back into the mists of

history, where we are able to see along with him the internal strife, the surrenders, the twists and turns as well as the resistance. We can also see the fragility and complexity of life along with the bleeding details that make up the great events of the time. His words burn with a pure blue flame, detailed and straightforward, infused with the intuitions of an artist and the wisdom of a philosopher. He told me that he has to suppress a colossal anger when he writes, but I could not sense this at all. Clearly he possesses the profound skill to funnel his life's fury into strings of words.

We set out from Manhattan to visit the Gaos, driving through the Holland Tunnel into New Jersey. My friend Xueliang drove a tiny, decrepit car he had borrowed from his brother. Even the new tires had problems, and the car wobbled as we drove. As we left the metropolis, we passed through open country that became ever more sparsely populated, and which the spring wind had just turned green.

They'd purchased a small house in a retirement community in southern New Jersey for $50,000, a sum that would have hardly been enough to purchase a bathroom in Manhattan. I had once been a construction worker, and I could see instantly that the house was built of cheap materials. It had a living room and two bedrooms, one of which was used for sleeping and the other as Gao's study. There was also a light and spacious greenhouse, which Xiaoyu used as a studio. It was vastly quiet there, so quiet that your ears rang.

They lived simply, with little contact with others. Aside from painting and writing, their only amusement seemed to be hiking in the nearby woods.

Gao Ertai was different from any other Chinese intellectual I had ever met. He looked like a farmer with his squinting eyes and ruddy face, which always had on it an open smile, as if he had just seen a good harvest. As I spoke with Gao, Xiaoyu continued with her "translation." I eventually found out I was sitting in the wrong place, as I was talking into his deaf left ear, so I moved over to be next to his right ear, which made it much easier to converse. It suddenly occurred to me that he didn't wear a hearing aid, which seemed a clear signal that he was intent upon cutting off his connections to the world. By closing one door he was able to open another, the one leading to the interior.

I praised his essays and this time he heard me; he was as happy as a child and asked me what other people thought of his work. He went back and brought out a photo album from his study, except that instead of photos, the pages were full of bits of yellowing paper only a bit bigger than matchbook covers. When I looked carefully at the papers I saw that they were covered with characters as fine as the hairline cracks on ancient pottery and were almost impossible to read with the naked eye. He told me that each slip of paper had over ten thousand characters on it, and that he had written them while in the reeducation camp. For safety's sake he had ground down the nib of his fountain pen until it was finer than a needle. He had used the moments when no one was around to write on these slips of paper, and then hidden them in the lining of his padded jacket. His jacket ended up with more than a dozen of these containers of various sizes, which he had stuffed full of dangerous secrets. When they came to search his house during the Cultural Revolution, they confiscated all of his manuscripts, but these little pieces of paper, full of thoughts even more secret, were ignored through their inattention.

After dinner he took me to see the paintings he and Xiaoyu had done. Their lives were not easy, so last year the two of them had made thirty paintings for the temple. In the 1960s he had spent a number of years copying wall paintings in the Dunhuang research center, and clearly God had been watching out for him, as it was his skill at this type of painting that became his means of making a living when he went abroad. He told me that whenever he thought about making a living writing, he would very reluctantly put down his pen.

In the corner of the living room stood a homemade wood frame for doing pushups. I visited the gym regularly to work out and felt pleased if I could do twenty pushups in a row. He, on the other hand, was able to do fifty without breathing any harder or breaking a sweat, and all this at age sixty-two. In the 1950s he tied the national record in the hundred-meter dash. Maybe a creator had provided him with this powerful consti- tution so that he could endure past the endurance of others and bear witness to the world's misery. He told me that when he was put in jail after June Fourth, an inmate had mistreated him in the same way that all newly arrived prisoners were mistreated, and that he just couldn't put up with anymore, so he flattened the guy with a couple of punches and a kick.

Gao Ertai brought out a jar of the finest rice wine. During dinner, Xiaoyu continued to echo everything we said. When it came time for us to depart, Gao took our hands and said in a loud voice, "I'm very happy you came!" With that, he restored the original significance to this tired phrase: he really was happy.

It had grown dark and we took the wrong road out, which led us right back to the house. The two of them were still standing there, probably preparing for their walk. I watched them, walking hand in hand through the moonless woods, toward the dawn.

ONE-WAY CONNECTION

Yu Yong is a pseudonym. This is to prevent the American INS or a particular police department in China from causing trouble for him. Actually, I've never met him, and know almost nothing about him. The only thing I am familiar with is his heavy northeastern accent.

One day last fall my wife Shao Fei suddenly received a phone call from a stranger. "My name is Yu Yong, and you probably haven't heard of me, but my father went to grade school with your mother, and that's how I got your number." He went on to tell bits and pieces of his personal story. He had made a bit of money back in various parts of China, dealing in futures and liquidating bankruptcies. Last year he had gone to Canada to try his hand at business there, but without success, so he slipped across the border to the United States. He originally planned to start up his own business overseas, but he hadn't counted on the Canadian economy's being so weak, and ended up only spending rather than earning any money. He then came to the States because someone told him it was easier to make money here.

"Fuckin' USA's hardly any better than Canada." He got increasingly more angry as he told the story. Shao Fei asked him where he was then. "In San Francisco. My Canadian visa's expired. Isn't it supposed to be an unregulated border?" He finally revealed why he had called — that he hoped to be able to come stay with us, and that we could help him find work.

"I'll do anything." Shao Fei asked for his phone number. "I don't have one. I'm calling from a pay phone with a phone card." It seemed as if our connection was destined to be one-way.

We had just been through an unhappy period in our lives, and we really didn't have the courage to deal with a stranger as remote from us as he was. The fact that he had haunted the commercial sphere in the way he did made us even more wary. For his part, Yu Yong used his own special way to enter into our lives. He was the initiator of our one-way contact, only calling us when a significant turning point happened in his life. Someone told him that it was possible to make money in New York, so he went there. "This place is not so great" was his judgment of New York: "The streets are packed with cars, the tall buildings are all too dark, and the air is vile. There are too many black people and it's dangerous. It's hard to find work, and if you don't have the proper papers, the employers won't even look at you." The intelligence reports he submitted got briefer and briefer, and the situation seemed to be turning grim.

In April, he suddenly asked us to lend him money. "I just can't live in America anymore." He began to stutter, "I, uh, am planning to return to Canada. Can you, um, lend me some money for the trip?" Shao Fei came to discuss it with me. We were, however, short ourselves at the time. We'd already bought plane tickets for the summer, and after paying the mortgage and the credit card bills, we had hardly anything left. But I knew how hard up I would have to be in order to ask for a loan, so Shao Fei and I told him that we would talk about it some more. But before we could give him the money, the initiator of our conversation had melted into the human sea. By now he was wandering the streets of San Francisco facing the sunset by the bay, depressed — the phone card tucked into his pocket was his only contact with the world.

Three weeks later we received another call. First there was a mechanical voice in English: "This is a collect call. If you wish to accept it, please press three, otherwise . . ." Yu Yong's desperate shout broke in: "Shao Fei! Press three right away, it's an emergency!" After she pressed three, he sounded like a drowning man who had finally made it back to the surface. "I've been in jail for seven days. I'm suffering; there are thirty men to a cell and the food is terrible. They only gave me back my address book today."

He had been washing dishes in a Chinese restaurant when the INS swooped down and raided the place. His boss received a heavy fine, and he was thrown in prison in Seattle, not far from the Canadian border. "You're the only people I know in the US. If you lend me four thousand dollars to make bail, I'll definitely return it as soon as I can. From having been a few hundred dollars for travel money, the sum he wanted had grown to four thousand for bail; where were we going to get that kind of money? "OK, OK, give my father a call and have my brother wire you the money, then you can mail me a check for the amount. I have to appear in court before the 29th of the month and if I can come up with bail, I can apply for political asylum." He then raised the issue of his buddies in Vancouver who could set up an exhibition of Shao Fei's paintings. It hardly seemed like the time to bring this up. When she asked him his phone number, he replied that the jail had a phone with neither a dial nor a number, and that he could only make collect calls. Our pattern of communication had not changed.

When this all happened I was in Narita airport waiting for my connecting flight back to the United States, eating a bowl of noodles in the snack bar on top of the building. Next to me were two young women from Taiwan who were discussing the exchange rate between yen and dollars, planning to buy a bottle of XO for their father in the duty-free shop. On the other side of me was a Chinese couple who appeared to have lived in America for some time. They were scolding two very young children. "Tell me the truth, who shoved the table?" said the mother in a severe tone. The father nudged her, "Use English." So the mother repeated in English: "Who shoved the table?" The United States was our common destination.

Whether an immigrant is legal or not depends on the times, one's friends, and money, not to mention luck and a host of other matters having to do with the interpretation of the law. Everyone in America except for the Native Americans is an immigrant; it is only a question of whether people arrived earlier or later. If one approaches the matter from the perspective of *natural right*, then everyone should have the right to choose where on the earth one will live — this is the freedom of movement. Yu Yong was thrown into jail for exercising this freedom.

Since there was only a week between the time of Yu Yong's signal for help and his appearance in court, Shao Fei tried calling his father that night but couldn't get through. The only thing she could do was to send a message to him via my mother-in-law. Early the next morning Yu's father finally returned the call, speaking in a bleak northeastern accent. Aside from expressions of concern and gratitude, he firmly assured us that Yu Yong had absolutely no political problems back at home. The old guy just couldn't understand that this was a Chinese convention — that if you didn't have political problems, then you were able to join the party or to be promoted — but that the American standard was set up so that he could only stay if he did have political problems back at home. The old father, who had endured so many political upheavals, couldn't get himself around this notion. Four thousand five hundred American dollars was eventually wired from Manchuria, but it took a number of days to arrive. Yu Yong called almost every day, extremely expensive collect calls, which I am told cost five times as much as an ordinary call, but one must allow the drowning the chance to surface and take a breath. Shao Fei was on her way to Malaysia to open an exhibition of her paintings, so the burden of rescuing Yu Yong fell on my shoulders.

On May 28th, the day before Yu Yong was supposed to appear in court, I discovered that the money had arrived when I went to make a withdrawal at an ATM. I went immediately to the bank, wrote a cashier's check, and then rushed to the post office to send it special delivery. The postal worker guaranteed that it would arrive before noon the next day. The young Asian man behind the counter glanced at the address, which had only a box and dormitory number, and asked quizzically: "Are you sure he'll be able to sign for it? If he can't, then they'll send the letter back." He had experience with this sort of thing, so I checked off the right of the recipient to receive the letter without signing for it. When I got back home, Yu Yong surfaced again, and I told him the good news.

The next afternoon he called and told me in a dejected voice that he had not received the check. All the Chinese in the jail had left and he couldn't speak English, so he couldn't talk to the guards. He was resourceful in a crisis, however, and asked me to hold on while he went to get one of the guards. After a very long time, an extremely thick Russian accent appeared on the other end of the line. I was thoroughly perplexed — had the Russians taken back this American prison? I assured him that the money must have arrived, and asked him to go check, and then to release Yu Yong. He told me there was nothing he could do, which made me angry, so I asked him who was really in charge? The phone went back to Yu Yong, who explained that he had been unable to find a guard, so he had asked a fellow Russian inmate to come to the phone. I wasn't sure how to piece it all together. I did learn from the Russian that bail was $2,500, instead of $4,000. "That's great, because money's just about better than anything else these days." He was excited and changed the subject: "Were you just watching the NBA finals? Those Bulls are really something . . ."

Yu Yong didn't get hold of the check until a week later. I couldn't sue the post office since they had delivered the check to another world, much less sue the prison, since I really didn't know Yu Yong, and might have had to change places with him on suspicion of being the "snake head" who had originally smuggled him in. During these few days he continued to articulate to me his anxiety and anger, and even as I was expressing my sympathy, I worried about this month's telephone bill.

After another ten days, Yu Yong was given his freedom, and he used a phone card to call me from Seattle's Chinatown. He had two thousand dollars in his pocket, so his voice had become a bit more resonant.

"We've become such good pals that there must be something that keeps bringing us together; sooner or later we're going to sit down and have a good talk." I asked him about his plans for the future. He said that his day in court had been put off until the day after tomorrow, and that after he got political asylum, he could at least stay here legally. And after that?

If nothing worked out he could always go back to Canada. "An expired visa doesn't matter," his voice took on the tone of a battle-hardened veteran: "Isn't it an unregulated border?"

ANA BLANDIANA AND A GROUP OF SOUTH AFRICAN SCHOOL CHILDREN

Journey to South Africa

The flight from New York to Johannesburg is fourteen hours.

I sat by the window. A hulking white man was caught between me and a black woman sitting on the aisle. He conversed with the woman for a while before he turned toward me. He turned out to be an employee of a South African bank and lived in Johannesburg. He was not satisfied with the situation in South Africa after the change in government in 1994, "You know, we still have the same crisis as before." When he asked about me, he concluded, "you must be going to the same conference that she is." He took a breath and cleared some space so the two of us could talk. The woman was named Lorna, and she had a wide face and generous mouth, which gave her a jubilant look. I drank South African red wine as I looked over the materials sent by the poetry festival. Lorna was from Jamaica, Jamaica is in the Caribbean, the Caribbean is on the earth, and the earth is in the universe . . . .

When I woke up I was being suffocated. The hulk's whole body had gone slack when he had fallen asleep, and he was now oozing out of his seat. I began to meditate to ward off the fear of confinement.

In Johannesburg, we had a more than three-hour wait for our connection. In the snack bar I ran into Lorna who was drinking tea; I had mango juice. We were both so tired that we could think of nothing to say to one another. I asked whether or not she had noticed how few black people there were among the travelers. She responded that black people liked to stay on the ground. But Lorna, from Jamaica, flew all over. She doesn't live in Jamaica, but in the United States where she teaches creative writing at the University of Michigan. I had lived there myself. She suddenly forgot the name of someone she knew well and became distracted, with a look of being at a loss. She was sure that after a good sleep she would remember the name.

By the time we reached Durban it had already become dark. Durban is South Africa's largest port city, with over a million people. With its trailing palm trees and British colonial architecture, it is a tropical dream of empire. Along the oceanfront stand the sorts of hotel one can find all over the world. We stayed at the *Blue Water*. Looking out the window I could see layer after layer of white waves driving toward shore through the dark. The organizers had warned us not to go out alone after dark, as the crime rate in South Africa was reported to be six times higher than New York. I returned to the lobby where Lorna was already sitting, and we were taken to a nearby Italian restaurant for dinner.

My old friend Breyten hugged me tightly. I call him "Jesus," not just because he looks like him, but more important, because of his calm and compassionate eyes. He spent seven years in prison in this country, and lived in exile in Paris for even longer. It had fallen to him to organize the poetry festival.

Breyten is a painter in addition to being a poet, and unfortunately I had just missed the opening reception for an exhibit of his paintings. He introduced me to each of the poets in attendance.

A tall, thin black man burst in. It was Hawad, the nomadic poet of the Sahara. We had met ten years before at a poetry festival in Rotterdam. At that time, he had sported a cloak and sat on the floor in the lounge, summoning souls and exorcising ghosts. This time he was wearing a short coat — a Chinese style blue jacket with cloth buttons. His English was limited, so he only pointed to the jacket and said: "Paris, I buy, very cheap." He then followed with a rush of French that I couldn't understand at all. That was his style — he had lived among camels for many years.

I sat beside the Canadian poet Patrick, and beside him was the Dutch poet Jules. Across from us was Patrick's companion Lorna (another Lorna). Patrick told me that when he had visited China in the early eighties as part of a delegation of Canadian writers, he was continually surrounded by people who pointed at his nose and shouted out: "Norman Bethune, Norman Bethune." He does actually resemble Bethune, with his wide forehead and balding head, but his facial expressions differ completely. In contrast to the steadfast communist warrior, Patrick lacks zeal and has a more skeptical look about him; he is a Bethune who has survived the atomic age. By the time he got to Beijing he was weary of the official arrangements and wanted to get in touch with those of us who were rebelling against the orthodoxy. The Writers Association continually evaded his requests. With the help of his interpreters, however, he was able to make contact with some young local poets when he reached Xian.

The Canadian Lorna and the Dutch Jules were arguing heatedly over the movie *Titanic*. Lorna rejected it completely: "Trite, sentimental and completely worthless . . ." "What?" Jules cocked his head: "That was pure passion! When di Caprio stood on the prow of the ship," Jules puffed out his chest and made as if to fly, "Don't you understand? The passion of life!"

Only then did I notice his appearance: the long face, the

tips of his mouth pointing down, oily, slicked back black hair plastered to his head. He was outfitted completely in black — glasses, suit, even a black clip-on tie — which made him look exactly like an Italian Mafioso. I made up my mind to stay as far away from him as I could during the festival.

The next morning I sat next to the Romanian poet Ana. We realized we had previously missed a chance to meet one another in the spring of 1986, in a little theater at London's Covent Garden. The convener, Michael, had announced that due to unexplained reasons, Ana had not been able to get an exit permit and would not be able to attend the poetry reading. Twelve years later our lives had changed dramatically: in 1986 she had wanted to leave her country but could not, while in 1998 I wanted to return to mine but could not.

In the hotel lobby I ran into Hawad. I had always wanted to clear up the matter of his nationality, but this question always seemed to irritate him. "I have no country; I only have a homeland — the Sahara. Dammit! My desert has been divided up among four different countries." He made a vow that one day he would evade the border guards of those four countries and take me to his Sahara Desert. Trust me, he said as he thumped his thin chest. I remembered that he had said the same thing a decade ago.

"The Saharan" pulled a fountain pen from an embroidered leather bag, and, through a combination of pictures, complicated hand gestures, and the scribbling of single English words,

149

described his ethnicity. The Berbers are Moslem nomads who have consistently been displaced by national conflicts and thus have no country of their own; their ancestors originated in the Gobi Desert of northwestern China. He patted my shoulder: "You, I, both Orientals." I gave him a puzzled look. They did indeed have their own writing system in which his poetry was written, and when he wrote it down, it did look a bit like Chinese, and part of me actually began to believe that I might be distantly related to this wild, curly-headed black man.

At five o'clock in the afternoon we gathered in the lobby of the hotel and got in jeeps to go to the theater of the University of Natal. The Saharan sat himself down on the terrace outside the lobby, spread his arms out and began to chant. I asked the French woman, Maud, who was responsible for the interpreting, exactly which spirits he was invoking. Maud shrugged her shoulders: "he's not using French."

Over the past decade the Saharan had aged manifestly; perhaps the spirit of the desert had grown weary of the refined cultivation of the French language and thrown him aside. The last time we met he never seemed to stop, always in control of a limitless energy.

The Jamaican Lorna shouted my name, then broke into laughter without saying any more. She seemed to have relaxed to such an extent that just saying my name made her giddy.

The bell rang and the house filled up. A group of young black men rushed up on stage, slapped their feet and began to dance: the expression of African hospitality. The second African poetry festival began to the sound of this fast-paced rhythm.

II

The poets quickly broke up into small groups. Each day when we got in our vehicles, these irrational divisions, mostly based on language, could be seen. For transportation we had two red Toyota jeeps as well as the small white car of Maud, the French translator. The English group consisted of "Norman Bethune" and his partner, the Dutch "Mafioso," the South African poet Ingrid de Kok, and myself. Our van was always packed, as we were sometimes joined by Ana and the Indonesian Rendra and his wife. There were only three in the French group, the French poet Bernard Noël, the Moroccan poet and novelist Tahar Ben Jelloun, who lived in Paris, and the nomadic Saharan.

They all crammed themselves into Maud's little car. Thus did this arrangement reflect the unhappy position of the French in the struggle for linguistic hegemony. I have no idea why the world has turned against the French language, and there is perhaps no blame to be assigned. Fortunes constantly change, and perhaps some day the whole world will end up speaking Chinese.

I had encountered Tahar before, at the 1990 International Writers' Conference in San Francisco. I tried to chat with him on the day of the opening of the festival, but he hemmed and hawed as his wife stood icy guard. I remained there awkwardly holding my drink in my hand, finally using my only word of French, "Bonjour" with which to beat a retreat.

But when it came to the speeches at the meeting, no one else could get a word in. Every member of the French delegation spoke with alarming fluency, and with plenty of theory thrown in for good measure. At the meeting on human rights, Tahar presented us with the latest definition of individualism, and the Saharan exhorted us to resist American cultural imperialism from a position of anarchism. Bernard, who had been seated in the audience, rushed on stage to deliver a long pronouncement on liberty. He employed a characteristically postmodern rhetorical style: each new term pushing aside the term before, like some animal trying to cover up its tracks, until at the end you had no idea where he had begun. I began to refer to him as "the philosopher." All I recall now is his pallid face and his hands trembling with emotion. The eloquence of the coffee house coupled with the metaphysics of wine.

The last five minutes of the meeting were set aside for me. I had grown sick of vacuous words about human rights and gave voice to my agreement with the natural anarchism of the Saharan. After we adjourned, he took tight hold of my hand and once again assured me that someday he would take me back to the desert. For my part, I agreed to go back with him to have a look around his ancestral home — the Gobi Desert.

My attempts to avoid the "Mafioso" were futile, as we were bound up in the same group, in spite of the fact that English was the native tongue for neither of us.

Aside from giving readings in the evening, we went to visit high schools during the day. For two days running I went to private girls' schools. They were almost too orderly, with an air of the British aristocracy permeating them. The girls all seemed like uniformed angels, as if they spent all their time playing the flute, plucking the harp, and singing hymns. There was a large number of Indians and Blacks among them. In South Africa, the racial issue has receded in importance: all are equal according to their wealth. The tale of several hundred years of colonial rule has suddenly come to an overly simplistic conclusion. But when a teacher ordered an older black worker to move a slide projector, I could see the unease in his eyes, the unease of several hundred years' endurance.

At the very same time we had gone to heaven, another group of poets had descended into hell — a library in a poor district of Durban, where their audience was a group of young African children dressed in rags. "Norman Bethune" told me later that the strangest thing they noticed was the lack of a single book in the library.

The next day I went with the Canadian Lorna and Rendra to read before another group of angels. Lorna and I opened the program. Lorna was a natural teacher, and the students immediately took to her. Most of her poems had to do with love, and the audacity of her wording made me blush. She had won all of the important literary prizes in Canada, but many schools forbade the teaching of her poems. I warned her that she should under no circumstances read her erotic poems, so she read a poem about love among onions. Rendra was the last to go. He declared that in Indonesia, poets are the equivalent of sorcerers and he did indeed declaim his poetry in a highly ritualistic manner. His thin wife said little, and kept her camera focused on her husband at all times, as if she were afraid his incantations might make him disappear. Rendra finally invited his wife onstage where they embraced one another and tenderly sang a love duet. The stage lights darkened.

I knew Gert, a South African poet and singer. He was a young man from a remote rural area, and arrived two days late. Jesus told me that when he had driven to the airport to get Gert, the young man had been thrown into a panic, "I would never have dared to imagine that a man as great as you would come to pick me up . . . . " Jesus replied with a laugh, "There is no hierarchy among poets."

I went out with Gert. He had a scruffy little beard and wore a jacket of rough cloth that revealed his powerful arms. While I shopped he sat in a coffeehouse writing a letter to his girl friend. This was the first time he had been so far away from home. He pointed out his home to me on a map — a little town in the middle of South Africa that he asked me to visit the next time I came. "Life there is very different," he said. He looked at people in a highly peculiar way, with eyes narrowed, looking directly at you, half cunning, half perplexed.

We had lunch together in an Indian fast food place. He had worked as a waiter, a doorman and a bouncer in a bar — "I look pretty strong on the surface, but I'm actually completely lacking in courage; I'm always ready to run when things get rough." He didn't speak much English, and even that little bit was difficult for me to understand. He had become popular as a singer over the last couple years and had even put out a CD. The Rotterdam poetry festival was planning to invite him to read this same year. When we talked about this, his eyes went blank for a moment.

The poetry festival proceeded smoothly. Before their readings, the poets bought one another drinks and made jokes. The English and French groups invariably stayed within themselves. I thought of the words of R.S. Thomas: *if the various peoples of the world had never encountered one another, they would all have led much easier lives, with great stretches of water separating them.*

Perhaps he was right, as contact has given rise to new kinds of conflict, new controlling desires do give rise to new kinds of pain.

The Jamaican Lorna pulled me aside; she was collecting contributions for a gift for the organizers of the festival.

The Saharan stood on the terrace reciting a speech into the darkness: that damnable American culture, which used the Yankee dollar to occupy the world. My home! — he shouted at the top of his lungs. The Mafioso had changed into black glasses and a white tie, and made the following evaluation of the Saharan: "He's idealizing his desert. Why does he live in Paris and never return to his beloved desert?" Jesus knitted his brow and said, "Idealizing our native places is a problem for us all."

The Mafioso was easier to comprehend on stage than in real life; his poems were black, like his apparel.

Patrick's poetry was, like that of his companion, Lorna, packed with erotic elements, including numerous descriptions of sexual organs. The two of them treated poetry as if it were a mirror in their bedroom.

Before he read, the philosopher announced his poetic manifesto.

Gert gripped his guitar as he went on stage and readied his harmonica harness. His voice was loose and a bit hoarse. A projector simultaneously transmitted a collection of photographs on the screen, some of him with his family, some of a railroad reaching out toward the empty horizon, others of city lights. They were all concerned with the gentle sorrows of a country youth and his melancholy at leaving home, and at the same time hinted at his longing for distant parts.

We had dinner at an Indian restaurant. I had had a good deal to drink, and began singing the Indonesian folk song "Singsingso" for Rendra and his wife, the Romanian folk song

"Captain Gheorge" for Ana, the "Red River Valley" for Patrick, and together with Jesus sang "The Internationale."

III

Suffering from jet lag, I went to sleep early, but turned on the television at six the next day to catch the CNN morning news. Indonesia was in political crisis, with the student movement in peril of being suppressed at any moment. The deeply concerned Rendra and his wife took center stage at the breakfast table. They had not been able to get through by phone, and all five of their children were involved in the movement, with one actually taking a small leadership role.

Rendra, moreover, was regarded as one of the spiritual leaders of the country, and was in danger of being imprisoned or refused entry when he returned home.

The Jamaican Lorna told me that she planned to buy a bunch of roses to present to the organizers.

The Saharan had an upset stomach, announcing that it was from eating Western food. I wondered what he ate in France. He became taciturn and took on a dejected expression, shaking his index finger: "No good."

As our jeep drove past a cemetery, the Mafioso suddenly began to tell us about his cousin Annie. "I was still very young, and it was the first time I had ever seen this cousin who had

just come to visit us from South Africa. She was tall and pow-
erfully built, with an enormous pair of breasts. She embraced
me with all her strength, coming close to suffocating me, and
since then I have always been afraid of that part of a woman's
anatomy. My mother had her stay in my sister's room. Annie
was full of curiosity and looked all around when she came in
the room. My sister's room was full of posters of jazz musi-
cians, and Annie suddenly rushed out if it screaming: "Where
did you get all those niggers?" My mother was so angry she
shouted back: "Who do you think you are? Get the hell out of
here, you animal!" Annie was driven out and never came back;
nobody knows what ever happened to her. It's been so many
years, maybe she ended up buried here . . . . "

We went to an area inhabited by the poor. Having been
abroad for so long, there were many things I had forgotten.
The scene shocked me: the fierce sun, the dust, the huts of
corrugated iron, the rags on the children and the crude and
shabby cemeteries. Single men and women lived separately in
two old gray buildings, having come from afar in search of
work, like the itinerant workers in China. A third building
was covered with drying diapers, an emblem of marriage, which
brought warmth to hopeless lives. As our guide explained what
we were seeing, a cow strolled into the middle of the road and
defecated, waved its tail and lazily walked off.

Only a few miles away we came to a spotless modern city
with a strange name: New Germany. "Aha, I like this name,"

shouted out the Mafioso, "Two years ago a damned German ambulance ran into me. My whole face was covered with blood and I still haven't been able to get the blood out of my shirt."

I don't know why, but I was starting to like this guy. I discovered that underneath his Mafioso-like exterior lay a soft and sentimental heart. Regardless, he was the sort of eccentric one rarely encounters, with his collection of eight thousand 78-rpm jazz records, his eighty pairs of dark glasses and fifty black suits. While he wore his dark glasses at all times, his evaluations of people and events were pretty much on the mark. I asked him why he wore his glasses at night, and he replied instantly: "There is no reason to see things too clearly. When we judge people it shouldn't be on the basis of their appearance, but on their actions."

We arrived at a library in a poor district, a plain empty building of five rooms, with only a dozen shelves of books in one of the rooms. A television mounted on the wall was in the midst of broadcasting a Chinese kungfu movie. The Saharan disregarded his illness long enough to once again commence with his attacks of American culture: "Look, the media are everywhere, and what sponsors it? The Yankee dollar! Shit, our homelands are being destroyed by the Yankee dollar . . . ."

A local black author told us that six years before the shelves in the library had been completely empty. He and his friends had gone out to raise donations, and had also contacted the authorities, actions which had given them the books they now had. They read their own poetry. The Saharan jumped up and accompanied them with shouts and movements that resembled the rebellious dances of the Cultural Revolution. At my request, the Canadian Lorna read her poem about onion love. The Mafioso read his dark poetry.

Eight or nine young black girls were changing their clothes in the courtyard. I took a photo of them as we went into the library and the girl at the end raised up her skirt, playing the coquettish movie star. When the drums sounded, the troop's coach gave a shout to which everyone responded. They kicked their legs in the air, did somersaults and made a pyramid, all of which looked extremely difficult. Ingrid, the South African poet, told us that the devotion to technique in African dance was extraordinary, with groups often rehearsing to the point of real physical pain, and where competitions are often seen as life and death matters. The drums suddenly stopped and, following a hand movement from the leader, the troupe scrambled after him into a car, their arms sticking out the windows like two banks of oars.

We returned to the "civilized world" and sat under umbrellas on the lawn of a hotel sipping beer and watching the undulating African mountains. Ana, who was sitting at our table, was recognized by three Romanians sitting nearby. She was dragged off to pose for a commemorative photo. Ana told us that she doesn't dare walk down the street in Bucharest, as throngs of people would surround her.

The sky darkened and a rain squall came upon us, driving all the poets into the hotel but not before soaking us all.

The next morning I ran into Rendra, who told me the situation was murky, with the students and the police facing each other in the streets. Suharto had cut short an overseas visit and rushed home to Jakarta. The army had been mobilized, but the chief of staff had promised not to repress the people. Pleased with himself, Rendra revealed that the chief of staff was a faithful reader of his work. In fact, he added, many people looked forward to his return.

The Jamaican Lorna wore a purple dress as she clutched a large bouquet of roses and happily asked everyone to sign a card. The card expressed our best wishes to the organizers and Lorna seemed to treat her sacred mission as the very reason she had made the long journey.

Jesus had flown to Zimbabwe first thing in the morning to attend a cultural activity. He had left a poem written to me, which he asked Patrick to read for him.

This was to be the closing ceremony of the festival, and each poet was to go on stage. The organizers stressed, however, that each poet was to be limited to one poem, the shorter the better, and in no case to exceed three minutes. The poets all went up on stage singlefile.

When the Moroccan Tahar's turn came, he spoke briefly in pure and correct English before reading, completely shocking me and Patrick: Tahar knew English! Language is certainly a concealed weapon in its ability to catch people off guard.

The last in line was Rendra, who clutched a great bundle of manuscript pages. He announced that he had been in the grip of an upsurge of emotion over the past several days, and had not been able to sleep, to which this poem gave testimony. The English "O fantasy" appeared in the first line, but all the rest was in Indonesian. He really did seem to be a sorcerer now, throwing each page up into the air after he had finished reading it. Apart from the occasional repetition of fantasy, there was probably not another word that could be understood by anyone in the audience. He spoke hoarsely, and his eyes burned. I concluded that the matter of his country's fate had driven poor Rendra a bit mad, and that he was taking us for the enthusiastic throng that awaited him in Jakarta. After he had read for a full twenty minutes, he was still grasping a whole handful of incantatory pages that he had yet to toss in the air. Patrick and I decided to withdraw, but just as we walked out the door, we heard catcalls, and Rendra hastily wound up his reading.

The Jamaican Lorna was finally able to present her roses.

After the curtain came down, the stage shifted to a restaurant where we all gathered. The next day we were scheduled to visit a game preserve, but only a few of us remained, as the majority were already going home.

In a corner of the restaurant was a singer. The Canadian Lorna got up and started to dance her way out into the street, taking a couple of young people with her that she hardly knew. The Mafioso brought a sixteen-year-old girl along with him, a girl who had been left out when the prizes had been announced in the high school poetry competition. During the period of autograph signing, the Mafioso had asked her to come along with us to dinner, and she had been delighted. Her father, on the other hand, furrowed his brow and looked him over with great care, only giving his grudging consent when the rest of us vouched for him. The Mafioso could not have been more courteous, encouraging her to keep writing, and inviting her to dance. He held his body as straight as a ruler, using his right hand to guide the girl around the floor, like a shadow stirring up the light.

Patrick commenced talks with the Philosopher of the French delegation through the mediation of an interpreter. Tahar was no longer speaking English, but using a paper napkin to plug his ears as he wandered about. He signaled me with his hands that it was too noisy. Maud told me that she had first written out the few sentences of English that Tahar had uttered on stage, and that he had had to read them many times before he could commit them to memory.

We requested Simon and Garfunkel's "The Sound of Silence" and "Bridge over Troubled Waters." Over the deafening music, the Saharan yelled: "This American garbage is an opiate for the spirit of the people . . . . "

Patrick told me that he and the Philosopher had hit it off

in their conversation; in fact, if not for the language barrier, they could have become good friends. This was the beginning of an accord between the English and French delegations, but it came too late, as the next day everyone was returning to his or her own territory, separated by a wide stretch of water.

IV

The next morning when I was checking out I ran into the Mafioso. He shook my hands and said gravely: "I don't need to give you my address, as you will always be able to find me whenever you are in Rotterdam." When he finished, he hurried to leave. Patrick told me that when the Mafioso had taken his leave, the latter had actually been in tears. The leaders of the French delegation came to the main door to see us off, and the farewell was harder than I had expected.

There were nine of us divided between two jeeps. After leaving Durban, we followed the coast for a time, eventually branching off to the northwest to head into the interior. I, Patrick and his companion, Maud, and the manager of the poetry festival, Gulam, were in one jeep, which Gulam drove. He was of Indian descent; a small capable man of about thirty who was primarily a business man, but also was in charge of numerous cultural activities, including the Durban International Film Festival.

Maud had been tormented by the Saharan into no longer being able to speak English, and fell asleep as soon as we got in the jeep. Maud was young, only twenty-six, and came from a small town in the vicinity of Lyon. She majored in African literature at the university and had volunteered to serve as interpreter for the festival. She seemed a bit strange, or, perhaps, it was a problem with me, as each time we tried to converse something always went awry and we ended up talking at cross purposes.

Hluhhluwe is located 280 kilometers from Durban, in Zulu territory. Founded in 1895, it is South Africa's oldest game preserve. Actually, the English word "game" has to do with hunting, and the original purpose of the preserve was to allow the animals to take their ease so as to get a better shot at them. Now, however, the meaning of the term has changed with the times, but, in any event, the animals didn't worry themselves with the vagaries of the interpretations humans had come up with.

Maud woke up when we entered the preserve. We held our breaths and looked all around. Lorna had the sharpest eyes, as she was the first to spot a giraffe, gracefully eating the leaves of a tree. We drove right up to it and it didn't budge, even when we got so close that we could hear it chewing. A herd of springboks crossed while a wild boar, immediately labeled Mr. Ugly, rooted around in a thicket. Gulam was as familiar with the animals as he was with the palm of his hand:

165

he pointed out the tracks of an elephant, the remains of animal bones in the spoor of a lion, and a mud hole used by rhinoceri for bathing. We eventually encountered two rhinoceri, right nearby. In their deliberate movements they seemed to care for nothing other than the grass they were eating, resembling two deep thinkers, except that they would never share their thoughts with the human race.

We spent the night at a hotel on a mountain. As it was fenced off on all sides, the place was safe, with each entrance fronted by metal pipes a certain distance apart that would cause the animals to either slip or trap their hooves. The hotel was made up of rows of small thatched huts as round as Mongol yurts. They were clean, but they had no toilets. We cooked steaks over a campfire, and drank red wine. Patrick and his companion helped out with the cooking, and I mad some Chinese food, which everyone pronounced satisfactory. When the two of us had enough to drink, Patrick and I sang "Red River Valley" together."

We had quite a lot in common: neither of us had attended college, and we had both been construction workers for quite some time. He and Lorna had lived together for twenty years. According to Patrick, "With no contract between us, every day is new." The two of them were a bit like children, first getting into a spat, then completely immersed in one another. Strangely enough, they never used a camera, for as Lorna said, "A camera's memory is entirely too limited."

A group of zebras had somehow sneaked in and were grazing near us. This seemed an ominous portent for the night: what if someone should run into a lion on the way to the toilet? I was the only one who had brought along an alarm clock, which meant that I had to knock on everyone's door at 4:30 in the morning. No one spoke as we drank weak instant coffee that was the same color as night.

We assembled at the main desk of the hotel and waited for quite some time before a man packing a rifle appeared and handed each of us a form. Looking at it carefully, I could see that it was a waiver, on which it was clearly written that in the event that we were carried off by an animal, the company could not be held liable. This came as a bit of a stimulant, but there was nothing to do but to sign on the dotted line.

Our guide Elliot was a short, thickly set Zulu. He loaded cartridges one by one into the chamber of his rifle, then swept his eyes over us and gave us brief instructions: everyone was to walk single file and make no noise; he would snap his fingers as a signal if necessary.

Should we run into an animal we were to remain calm and retreat, or take cover behind a tree, or disperse according to his hand signals . . . he reminded me of T.S. Eliot guiding us through our spiritual wasteland.

The eight of us closely followed the guide as we walked rapidly along an animal track; no one wanted to be left behind. In the past I had always had a problem with the term "closely follow," as in "closely follow the great strategy of Chairman Mao." Now I suddenly realized that to follow closely was mostly instinctive, arising out of terror.

The animal track and the way for humans resembled one another in their degree of peril — each allowed no room for mishap. Otherwise there would be no good end, as demonstrated by the spoor filled with animal bones.

I experienced for the first time the agony of shoes that were too small. Two days before I had been exploring Durban and picked up a cheap pair of sneakers, asked the size and was told they were just right. When I got back to the hotel I tried them on and they hurt immediately, as they were about two sizes too small. I had thought that my feet would stretch out the shoes, but several days later I learned how formidable the shoes were, especially at this critical time.

Elliot made a gesture with his hand for us to stop, but there seemed to be nothing but the rustle of the wind. We inched ahead several hundred feet when suddenly we spied three rhinos. We moved forward torturously according to his hand signals and then stopped; we were only about ten yards away. We confronted the rhinos, hardly daring to breathe. The rhinos probably summoned up some memory from deep within that humans were, after all, the more to be feared, and took flight. We had barely calmed down when the two Belgian women bringing up the rear reported that there was a rhinoceros closely following us. Elliot waved his hand in a sign that it was nothing to worry about.

We arrived at the edge of a small lake in the forest where we came upon several zebras drinking. They showed complete unconcern about our arrival and drank their fill before slowly going back into the woods. A number of weird and absolutely terrifying calls shattered the silence. We looked up but couldn't see anything, and figured it was probably just a vulture. In the course of these two hours, while wearing shoes that were much too tight and clutching my waiver of any responsibility for injury or death, I had begun to fear every new sound. But I eventually got used to things, even taking up a position at the rear, so as to show a bit of courage.

After returning to the hotel and thanking our savior Elliot, we felt joy at a kind of rebirth. For lunch in the hotel dining room, Maud, Patrick, his companion and I ordered braised venison; tearing at the meat with our own teeth, we could sense at least some of the ferocity of lions. During lunch, Patrick asked about Maud's family. "My mother died a month ago," Maud replied calmly. Patrick persisted with his questioning. Maud licked her lips: "she committed suicide."

Following an afternoon nap, Gulam drove us to an observation station. Surrounded by a tall log palisade, it resembled an ancient military encampment. We went in the front gate and through a large open space to a long corridor made of logs that were topped with wire mesh. At the end of the corridor was a sealed building like a fortress, but with a wide narrow window in the wooden wall. Outside the window lay an extremely tranquil pool surrounded by grayish-green woods. A family of wild boar with four or five piglets had come to drink. We could see the father disciplining a naughty son, squealing mightily as he chased the youngster around with his long tusks.

A man wearing an orange shirt came in and greeted us in French. Finding out that Maud was a compatriot, he launched into a constant stream of talk, which our whole party, including Maud, tried to hush. He sat for a while until he got bored and left in a huff.

A dusk descended that was so peaceful that we could only hear birds beating their wings and the noise of insects. A herd of gazelles came to water, then vanished into the woods. Three rhinos rumbled slowly up, breaking branches along their way. A small bird with a red beak sat on the back of one of the rhinos, as if it were an inspiration to the deep thinker.

On the way to the hotel a full red moon rose in the sky.

(FROM LEFT) PATRICK LANE, ELLIOT, BEI DAO, LORNA CROZIER, AND TOURISTS ON SAFARI AT A SOUTH AFRICAN GAME PRESERVE

CROWS

The town I live in is called Davis. There is nothing very special about it, as one can see from the postcards sold there: scenes of the ugly water tower, livestock at the university, the farmers' market; and if not these, then the town's trademark — an old fashioned bicycle, complete with an oversized wheel in front and small wheel behind, the kind first envisioned by da Vinci. It was welded together from steel pipes and stuck out on Fifth Street, the town's main artery.

But if you still insist on finding something special, there is one thing — the large number of crows.

173

In the United States I have found that people rarely look up at the sky. When they're headed to the office, their heads are buried in work, when driving or jogging or shopping they keep their line of sight leveled at the horizon. Heads are never raised in the manner of a character in a Chagall painting, looking back toward an attractive woman. When it storms, they watch the weather report and raise umbrellas as they go out the door.

Crows have a peculiar caw. In your car you can't hear it, and joggers with headphones tune out this particular channel of nature. Meaning that people only take note of their existence when the crows come in waves to deposit their grayish-green defecate. They gather together and ascend from trees in winter, covering the sky with their raucous sound like a scene from hell. I live in terror whenever I drive into town, and make every effort to avoid parking under a tree, but even then I can't seem to escape catastrophe.

I have heard that the city government has established a fine of $500 for killing a crow. But who could possibly have so little to do that he would want to make crow-meat noodles?

Every small town has its own personality. If you open up a map and gain the same viewpoint as a crow, you can see this clearly. Putah Creek represents our history, running by the southern edge of town.

Intersecting railroad lines partition the town into three equal segments, much like the predicament of civilization itself. The division of the center of town into a grid is clear, using numbers and the alphabet to name the streets, as if it were a preschool teaching letters and numbers. As the town expanded over the years, its mentality became more complicated: presidents, Indian tribes and the names of trees were used, along with the names of the earliest residents, who laid themselves down and gave themselves up to be streets. Chiles lies between the railroad and Interstate 80, never able to get a moment's peace.

Why Colonel J.B. Chiles decided to move to California remains a mystery to me. Perhaps it was his nature — some people are like house sparrows, never wanting to move their nests, while others are migratory. Between 1841 and 1854, the Colonel crossed the continent seven times between his Missouri home and the Sacramento Valley. With all of this upheaval he must have had stomach trouble. He was extremely thin, and looked like Abraham Lincoln with his eagle eyes and hooked nose. His ancestor, Walter Chiles, had also been a migratory bird, having sailed from England to Virginia in 1638.

In these days of clouds and constant rain, Putah Creek must be running full. I don't go out very much, only driving to the gym every other day. On one trip out I brought back two videocassettes. I am studying the history of our small town. In the beginning it was extremely tedious: dates, numbers, area, important events, births and deaths, but one day I suddenly got caught up in it and the scene changed. The characters took on life, as if they had been frozen but were now gradually thawing out under a bright sun. I became familiar with them and developed complicated emotional relationships.

Eventually it became all but impossible to distinguish between fact and imagination. For that reason, I will bracket material that emerged from my imagination in order to keep matters clear for you.

The notion that Sir Francis Drake first discovered California in 1579 now seems a bit ridiculous. Recent research indicates that the famous monk Faxian, of the Jin dynasty, landed near Seattle in 458 BCE, a thousand years before Columbus discovered America. And according to Professor Xu Songshi, most of the ancestors of the American Indians came from China. Four or five thousand years ago, following a flood of the Yellow River, they set out from the center of China and entered the North American continent via Siberia, the Bering Straight, and the Kuril and Aleutian islands. This thesis is also suspect, however, if only because of the clear contrast between the shrewdness of the Chinese and the honesty of the American Indians; but could not a culture of equal value have been produced on the new continent? Regardless of whose ancestors are whose, the Indians lived a nomadic life until the 1830s. The Patwin tribe lived on either side of Putah Creek.

If historians are judges, then crows are eyewitnesses to human migration, but since we can't interrogate them, we can't know any more than this.

Beginning in 1840, easterners began to move west. Their parties were a bit like tour groups today, consisting of thirty to fifty people and a guide. Colonel Chiles enlisted in the earliest ranks of these immigrants. The trip was a bit more miserable in those days, traveling on wagons without roads. And it wasn't just a matter of discomfort, because when they went over the mountains, they often had to sacrifice the wagons in order to save the people. Starting out from Missouri, it took half the year to reach California.

[No one ever wrote to the Colonel. He was severe in demeanor, and everyone was afraid of him. After being on the road for five hard months in the fall of 1841, they spent a night in the precipitous Sierra Nevada range. He missed his children, in particular Mary, his youngest, who was only six. His wife had died shortly after Mary's birth, leaving four children, and the Colonel had decided against every remarrying. Before leaving he had entrusted his children to relatives. When night came he returned to his tent and went to sleep. The wind blew all night.]

It is almost inconceivable how one can be turned into a city.

[J.C. Davis came west to work as a topographical surveyor. The money wasn't bad, and it was a chance to broaden one's horizons. He was tranquil as he set out on his journey, as he had nothing detaining him. He had grown up on an Ohio farm hating the cold winters and flat horizon. He had early on gone out in the world to do business, first running an inn. The Midwest was too conservative and he had no experience with love in his first twenty-three years. He was slow of speech but competent, and without any unrealistic expectations for life. There were numerous notions about California, such as there being gold everywhere, but he remained skeptical.]

Davis came to the Sacramento Valley at the end of 1845 and settled on the banks of Putah Creek. The next fall he served for two months in the army, on which point there is a discrepancy between the official documents and family records. His family members think that he was in the military for a much longer time, evidently holding it to be an honorable calling. At the time land was cheap, $1.25 an acre, less than a pack of cigarettes today. He and his father purchased 20,000 acres, with seven thousand of those enclosed by a fence. They had two thousand head of cattle, two hundred mules, six hundred sheep and one hundred and fifty pigs; in 1858 the farm was judged to be the finest in California.

[The crows came to roost in their trees.]

II

I got annoyed.

I went to the office on B Street that contained both the Chamber of Commerce and the Tourism Center. I rang the bell, and a young woman came out to greet me. After I explained what I was looking for, she directed me to a rack of brightly colored brochures, telling me I could take any that would help. They were all useless, so I asked her again. "Good question," she said as she began a search on her computer. She began to shake her head: "I'm sorry, but we don't have any material on the history of the town." I echoed her in an abridged form, "No history."

August 24, 1868, was a turning point for Davis: the Southern Pacific opened its first line. In the original plan the railroad was supposed to lie four miles west of the Davis farm, but it eventually went right through it. Aside from any influence father and son may have exerted, the main reason for this was probably consideration of the terrain in that they were trying to avoid marshland. Sometimes history is determined by place, otherwise Davis would have remained only a man and not become a city.

[When J.C. Davis entertained, he served only the finest Napa valley wines and roast venison. Among the three guests representing the railroad, the one with the mustache and the New York accent, who persisted in telling off-color jokes, was the most annoying. Davis knew, however, that he was the one who would make the final decision, and the mustached man drank himself into a stupor. As they were departing, Davis stuck an envelope in the man's pocket, in which were written figures he has never revealed to anyone.]

I drove to the California Railroad Museum in Sacramento. Brightly polished steam locomotives — relics of the modern age — attracted most of the attention of the visitors. Among the statues in the background are three Chinese laborers with *queues* down their back, moving rocks off a mountain. There is no written account at the museum of the fact that the Chinese provided most of the labor for the construction of the railroad. The historians behind the museum missed innumerable stories of the vicissitudes of life; the crows saw all but aren't telling.

The railroad brought instant prosperity to Davis. A man of the time left this account: "It is a well-ordered little town of five hundred souls. Olive Street is the main thoroughfare, which is packed close with wood-frame buildings, most of them one story in height. The town has a lumberyard, a wagon maker, stores and a barber, three hotels and a restaurant; it also has a stable, a saddle shop and a number of small markets. A church is under construction, which should be completed in the current season."

On October 2, 1869, the little town took its name from J.C. Davis.

By the 1870s, grain replaced gold as the main source of wealth in California. But who did all the work on the huge Davis farm? At first it was performed by Indians, but they were gradually replaced by Chinese. Once the work on the railroad was done, they were out of work, so they turned to farm labor. By the 1880s, there were thirty thousand Chinese coolies working in the Sacramento and San Joaquin valleys, providing almost ninety percent of California's farm labor.

[J.C. Davis learned a few expressions in Chinese, such as the words for "How are you?," "Eat" and "Work," as well as a few terms of Sinified English, like "Long time no see." He could order food in Chinese: "Chop suey."]

I can see the results of this linguistic exchange. At the weekend farmer's market I often see Chinese who have been hiding out behind the rows of crops for many generations coming to sell their produce. Aside from their inability to speak Chinese, they are just like the country people who come into Beijing and set up stands on the streets.

J.C. Davis set up the first cheese factory in the county and, along with Colonel Chiles and some others, established a rope-line ferry across the river; he was like the sun in the sky in these parts. He once paid sixteen dollars to Thomas the boat captain to work at night and take him across the American River to Colonel Chiles's home.

When word of this expenditure got out, people were astonished. Why did he go? The colonel had three daughters, and Davis was just one of many suitors.

[The first time Davis went to the colonel's house and saw his youngest Mary, she was still a little girl. But the passage of just a few years can change a person's perspective. The colonel was quite strict with his daughters, so Davis had few chances to speak with Mary. One night at a party at the colonel's house, Davis asked her to dance. He had had a bit too much to drink and his movements were stiff and awkward as a result, causing Mary to laugh out loud. The two of them slipped out into the back garden, and Mary's laughter attracted the attention of the colonel. His impression of Davis was generally favorable: taciturn but competent and intelligent. He sent someone over to investigate. Davis earned ten thousand a month from the ferry business alone.]

Davis married Mary in 1850. According to the 1850 census records, Davis was 27, a cheese maker from Ohio; Mary was fifteen and from Missouri.

Crows have a symbiotic relationship with humans. They are extremely fond of humans and dog our every footstep, eating and drinking what we leave behind. They also share the shortcomings of humans: they dislike being alone, always screaming out for company. They also have their own society, but humans can't be bothered to pay attention to it. As the saying goes, "All crows are black."

Looking at the statistical chart, I can see the growth of the town: in 1891 there were 700 people, in 1917 almost a thousand, in 1940 one thousand six hundred, and by 1950 there were suddenly nine thousand. This number has been further multiplied several times, so that now there are about fifty thousand. Following the appearance of the railroad, an agricultural school was founded in 1906, which later became a campus of the University of California, which is the main reason for the rapid population growth.

I had a bit too much to drink and roamed around in the dark, staggering a bit like a crow that has eaten fermented fruit. Our hero has been forgotten. I dare say that there are very few people in our town who know about him — his life, his joys and sorrows.

[He could never forget that day. The bright sun shining on Putah Creek, the windmill wheeling.]

Three year-old Amelia, only child of J.C. Davis and Mary, fell and mortally injured herself while playing at the mill while she was there with her father. Her brokenhearted father went mad and ripped apart the mill. Mary told people: "After the death of our child, we, as parents, could never again feel any sense of achievement."

Following years of drought and insect infestation, combined with the high tax rates following the Civil War, the farm spiraled into a decline. J.C. Davis eventually sold it off bit by bit and moved to Sacramento. In his later years he worked for the government, having been appointed street commissioner. He died October 5, 1881.

I have to confess that my research has not proceeded very smoothly, at least up to now. There are a number of reasons for this, such as a shortage of resources and my deficiencies with English. But the main reason is that the dead refuse to open up their inner beings. My voice has become somewhat peculiar, having a bit of the agitated tone of a cawing crow. The thought that I could attain something of the crow's lofty perspective has turned out to be an illusion.

CAT STORY

Almost fifteen years ago we had a cat we called Yellow Wind in our courtyard house in Beijing. He always liked to occupy the commanding heights and look down from the rooftops on our insignificant human lives, proudly holding his tail straight up in the air like a flagpole. I remember the day I brought him back from the office in my book bag and washed him. He burrowed his way down into the very bottom of our dresser, and when he finally poked his head out, we couldn't help but shudder: he looked to be the world's tiniest ghost. Yellow Wind's origins were untraceable, but we were certain he had been wild. He never showed any affection for home and would turn around and depart as soon as he had eaten, not showing up until he got hungry again. We lived in what was meant to be a five-courtyard house, but the courtyards had long since been filled up with jerrybuilt plank houses that had transformed the courtyards into so many alleys. Our little kitchen was at the far end of the last alley. When we made dinner in the summertime we would see Yellow Wind working his way back to us with his long tail high in the air. It looked as if he were inspecting the ranks of half-naked people lined up on either side of the alley trying to cool themselves off and, who, with their rush fans waving, recalled the palace honor guards of ancient times. Eventually Yellow Wind eloped with his lover, running away over the undulating rooftops and abandoning us.

A few years later I left Beijing. After enduring six years of the anxiety of separation, my daughter Tiantian and I walked through the streets of Paris discussing our future plans for a dog. This future had a particular immediacy for me, as I had just concluded living the unsettled life of a homeless dog.

Tiantian carefully evaluated all the dogs in Paris, and ended up not very satisfied. Finally she spied a Pekingese she liked that was hardly any bigger than my fist, tethered outside a beauty shop with a pink bowtie. The dog took turns barking and sneezing, as angry as a revolving fan. Tiantian couldn't resist going over and petting it, and ended up getting bitten.

I took Tiantian from Paris to the United States, and her mother joined us from Singapore. We settled in the small northern California town of Davis, where dogs were still a major topic of Tiantian's conversation. I took her to pet shops, consulted the want ads, and asked friends. One time after I'd returned from a trip to England, Tiantian blocked my way at the front door, and when she finally let me through, I focused on two newly born kittens. An advertisement for kittens up for adoption had fated these two little ones to end up here. To leap from dogs to cats is a bit like evolving from apes to humans, and contains so many imponderables that even God would not be able to explain. But this is the right of children, and no one follows their trains of thought.

Although the two kittens were brother and sister, they had nothing in common. The brother was strange in appearance: he was light brown, but had black spots all over his face and legs, as if he had stolen away to an inkwell to drink. The sister was an ordinary gray cat with black stripes. Tiantian and I racked our brains for names, finally settling on the mantra from the *The Lion King* that Tiantian repeated constantly: "Hakunamatata," which was then split into two and simplified: "Haku" and "Mata."

Haku was honest and straightforward by nature, and extremely adventurous. He was proud and content to pay no attention to people, but when he was bored and had nothing better to do, he would jump into your lap out of a pure curiosity to see how you ate, or wrote letters, or talked with people. Mata was careful and alert, ingratiating herself with people even as she was preparing to take flight at any moment. Her tail had a crook in it, probably caused by having had a door slammed on it when she was very young. This youthful trauma accompanied her throughout her life, and there would be no animal psychologists to explain to her exactly what a door was.

As soon as we got the cats, we began to keep the door to our rental unit shut at all times. Haku and Mata got themselves into trouble daily, whether it was urinating or defecating under the bed, upsetting the wastepaper basket or scratching our new Italian leather sofas; there was no way we could keep ahead of them. I took it upon myself to play cop, spanking them behind closed doors when there were no witnesses, or at least no one to report me to the SPCA. Whenever I went after the cats in a fit of anger, Tiantian held me back, crying and shouting at me, which allowed the animals plenty of time to get away. Sometimes another thought would cross my mind: if the kittens were a hundred times larger, they would be tigers, and Tiantian would be in the opposite position — pleading with them on my behalf.

Not long thereafter we bought a house, thereby liberating Haku and Mata, as we had someone install a cat entry in our front door. At first they were extremely wary in their explorations of freedom, but they eventually grew ecstatic. Behind our yard was an open field filled with golden wild flowers in which the cats jumped here and there, leaving two furrows like plows opening up virgin land.

Freedom, of course, has its costs. Friends told us that if the cats were going to be outside very much they needed to be inoculated against disease, and that a vet lived close by. Haku and Mata had a natural aversion to the smell of the veterinary hospital, which, with the sound of dogs barking added in, caused them to shake in terror and cry out piteously. When we got home, their eyes expressed even more fear and anxiety. Several months later I had them both neutered, an even more painful memory for them that caused them to stick even closer to me. I felt the guilt and loneliness of a dictator.

In the beginning, Haku was full of curiosity about the greater world and often wandered off. The phone would ring just as we were on the point of giving up our search, and it would turn out that Haku had grown weary and hungry in his peregrinations and had turned up on someone else's doorstep in search of food. Haku wandered even farther, and if he hadn't been attacked by a dog, he probably would have disappeared like Yellow Wind. One morning, Tiantian noticed that a big hunk of skin and fur had been torn off one of his front legs, revealing pink flesh underneath that was oozing blood. Haku didn't make a single sound of complaint, simply licking his wounds and coming to grips with the lesson transmitted to him by the dog: our world is a harsh place; from this point on Haku ceased his travels. He would sometimes go for a walk with us, but as soon as he detected a strange odor he'd run off.

After being neutered, Haku and Mata got even lazier and, aside from their three meals, spent all day sleeping. On the other hand, I was so busy I was always on the move, and would occasionally become envious of the cats' life and rather maliciously wake them up. They would open their eyes into narrow slits, as if fully comprehending my motives, and then turn over and go back to sleep.

If I were to compare them with Yellow Wind, I think the latter had a better life. The particular topography of Beijing's *hutungs*, the density of the population and local custom combined to bring him limitless sources of amusement. Neither was there anything as monotonous as manufactured cat food; back then we bought fish for Yellow Wind and prepared it for him ourselves. Haku and Mata, on the other hand, would at best condescend to sniff at fish, then turn up their noses and stalk off as their sense of taste had already atrophied. More important, however, was that their natural right to make love had been alienated from them. Few cats in Beijing are neutered and in the middle of the night the wailing of lovesick cats can be heard on all sides. Not to mention the fact that at the time it was not permitted to keep dogs in Beijing, so the world was a much safer place for cats.

Nevertheless, Haku and Mata were able to find ways to amuse themselves. They often dragged back crickets, dragonflies, small birds and mice. At such times the cats' yowling became most peculiar, and we were left to clean up the sordid consequences of their sadistic play. One morning I discovered a baby bird on the carpet calling out in hunger. Tiantian placed it in a little box lined with a handkerchief. The mother stood on a telephone wire in the backyard calling out in a desolate high C; Tiantian held up the box and said to her: "Here is your baby." We could not find the nest, but we did find another tiny bird, this one with cat teeth marks on it. We decided to try to raise the birds ourselves. They were pitiful looking: bald little wings, a few tiny feathers on their tails, long legs curled up underneath them, eyes tightly shut, but whenever they detected any movement, their mouths opened as wide as chrysanthemums.

"They're so ugly they're cute!" Tiantian exclaimed in surprise. We dug up some worms and they swallowed them right down, which led us to believe that there might actually be some hope for them. Tiantian's bedroom became the sickroom and we kept the door shut tight against the cats. By evening, one of the birds started to gasp for breath, and by morning both were dead. We held a funeral, burying them under a small grapevine in the backyard. That day we cooly ignored Haku and Mata.

From the back window I could see Haku stretched out on top of the wooden fence in the backyard, staring out into the distance. A bulldozer was leveling the ground, spewing out puffs of smoke into the air. The city was building a new park, and a park would surely draw more people walking their dogs. And all of those dogs, large and small, would certainly turn their heads our way and bark their way fanatically into Haku's nightmares.

DAUGHTER

Tiantian turned thirteen today. By a more rigorous count it actually should have been yesterday, since there is a sixteen hour time difference between here and Beijing. Last night I made spaghetti and poured her a small glass of red wine. "It's really sour," she said after taking a sip, then asked me, "Am I born yet?" I looked at my watch. Thirteen years ago at this exact moment she had just been born, and the nurse brought her out for me to see through a glass window. She had sparse hair and a completely red face, with saliva bubbles coming out her mouth.

There is deep significance to turning thirteen. As a teenager she can now go alone to PG-13 movies, go out by herself, and might fall in love at any moment. What bothers parents the most is the arrival of the second period of resistance. Psychologists think that the first period of resistance comes at about three years of age, when children achieve independence of movement. The second period comes at about thirteen or fourteen, with independence of thought.

Before I had made adequate mental preparation, the evidence of change was everywhere: she had begun to pay attention to what she wore, had her ears pierced, painted her nails, grew her hair to her shoulders and, like all American girls her age, became infatuated with *Titanic*'s di Caprio. Each and every one of them could sing the theme song. To avoid sinking beneath the tides of fashion, I even bought her a cassette of the movie's soundtrack.

Opposition in the realm of music began some time ago. Most of the time this presents no problem, as each of us closes our doors and listens to our own music. Last year, however, when we went to Las Vegas over Christmas vacation, her cassette with the high-pitched whining of Fan Xiaoxuan seemed completely out of control, and had an effect not only on my driving but on my sanity. If the police had ever played Fan Xiaoxuan's songs while interrogating me, I would have confessed to anything immediately. And similarly, when I put on my revolutionary songs, she plugged her ears and began to scream. Each generation has its own music, and never the twain shall meet. Music seems to be rooted in some physiological instinct; whenever I hear "Ode to the Spring Festival" I can taste rotting sweet potatoes, because in the winter of 1958, when the volunteers came back from Korea, the sweet potatoes piled up on our porch were molding. These two unrelated events are linked by the "Ode." As I sat on a bench gnawing at the sweet potatoes, the radio played it over and over.

For a Chinese in the West, the worst thing is loneliness; a deep sense of isolation. Americans understand this from the time they are born, but we Chinese must learn it. And it is a lesson that cannot be taught; everyone must experience it for themselves.

With no older mentors around, and without brothers and sisters, parents are never enough, busy as they are in a fog of middle-age activity. What can one do? After school, Tiantian comes home in a whirlwind, fixes herself a snack, flops on the floor, and turns on the television. Thus do the media turn a great mass of nonsense into laughter, using it to fill the gulf of silence that exists among people. Will Smith, the ebullient young man on the television, becomes a member of our family before my very eyes. Tiantian chuckles along with him as she does her homework.

But her favorite is still the Chinese series "I Love My Home." She has seen each of the 120 episodes in this series at least ten times and seems to have them all memorized. This is her attempt to find her roots, to seek out the pleasures of the Beijinger's garrulity, to seek out her geographical home, along with the struggles, entanglements and warmth of people from before her experience in America.

Last year during her summer vacation, Tiantian returned to Beijing, her geographical home. When she came back I asked her, if she could choose, where would she prefer to live?

She evaded the issue, and I eventually realized that it was a moronic question. If you have lived abroad for a long period of time, which country do you love? Even an adult would have a hard time responding. All one can do is waver between the two spots that have been labeled your home.

I took Tiantian to the pet store to choose a birthday present. She wandered around for a while, finally deciding on a small pet rat. I was absolutely opposed for two reasons. First, her mother is terrified of rats, and second, rats are terrified of cats and we already had two fearsome felines at home. Even if there were a cage between them, the cats would worry the rat into a heart condition, and we simply could not afford open-heart surgery for the rat.

Three weeks before, her mother had returned to Beijing to exhibit her paintings, so Tiantian and I were at home alone. Our schedules were at odds: she left for school early, before I woke up; when she got home I was just waking up from my nap; when she turned on the television I was going to the gym; when she was doing her homework I was at night school;

when I returned it was time for her to go to bed. Tiantian began to complain about my naps and trips to the gym; that my time at home was too short, and that most of that time was spent on the phone.

I had been separated from Tiantian for six years, from the time she was four until ten. During that time, while drifting around the world, I had thought through the matter and eventually realized that only Tiantian could serve as the anchor that would secure me. A friend living in England once told me that there was an old house in the country near him for sale at an unbelievably low price. He even dug out a photo to show me a dilapidated stone house surrounded by empty fields. This became my dream: I wanted no conflict with the world and to die in this foreign country. All I wanted was to raise Tiantian while catching the rye.

Last night I woke suddenly with Tiantian standing by my bed, her hands covering her eyes, muttering to herself. She had had a nightmare and dreamt of a vampire. I wondered if she hadn't dreamt of that old stone house. She had told me that she often dreamt of flying through the air. It seemed as if things were running opposite to my hopes: she wished to fly away and leave behind the endless fields of rye and the long shadow of her aging father.

Now that Tiantian has reached the first year of junior high school, her schoolwork has increased and I have to help her with her homework. Since I am completely hopeless at math,

I can only stumble my way through history with her. The history textbook is reasonably lively, so I end up learning along with her. We have recently entered the dark ages of the medieval period: The Black Death has wiped out a third of the population of Europe. The Bible has not yet been translated into the vernacular, so the power of interpretation remains in the hands of a small minority of priests who are using their hold on Latin to corrupt the church.

One day she told me that her history teacher had announced that if the five students who tested best paid five more dollars, their grades would be raised even higher. All the other students were dumbstruck, and then furious. Tiantian had taken a beating on the test, so she, of course, joined the ranks of the protesters. I went along with her righteous indignation: Rebellion is justified! But it turned out that we had all been duped, as the whole thing was only an exercise from the history textbook concerning Luther's Reformation.

Tiantian is without any great ambition. If you ask her what she wants to do, she'll eventually respond quite casually that pretty much anything easy will do. This is all right, as those of my generation were driven mad by lofty ambitions; our personalities were twisted into abnormal configurations with a serious tendency for violence. It is absurd to think of us actually saving a nation and its people when we did so poorly at saving ourselves.

The endless stories of agony in the former society that I have hated since my youth now fall to us to tell. Tiantian takes them in stride, simply walking away. How will the next generation live? That is a question they will answer.

One day I was awakened from my nap by a hard rain beating on the roof. My watch said 3:10, the time Tiantian gets out of school. I drove to the school, but couldn't find a parking spot, so I turned on the emergency lights, got out my umbrella and rushed inside. I met the students pouring out, opening their umbrellas one by one as they walked into the wind. I looked all over for Tiantian's red coat. The boys were thick-limbed and tough; the girls talked quickly as they moved along. I walked against the current, and very soon everyone had left and the building was empty. I turned around.

The rain had stopped and the sky had cleared.

A Day in New York

At five o'clock in the morning I am awakened by a helicopter flying directly past my window. The beginning of *Apocalypse Now* flashes into my head; a nightmare of the helicopter blade turning into the fan circling overhead. How does the pilot stay awake at five in the morning, navigating through skyscrapers in the changing light of dawn? As soon as the helicopter disappears a police siren starts up. First there is only one, followed immediately by a second and then a third, as if a soloist were summoning the remaining orchestra. This is the same music that always accompanies the ending of action movies: sirens blaring while the credits roll. There is a sigh and I sit up; it's the dog Fifi stretched out at my feet. What does a dog's sigh signify on the twenty-seventh floor of a reinforced concrete building?

Mimi, my hostess, is making breakfast. We are the same age. She is divorced and lives alone; her two sons in college are like eagles who return to the nest for brief stays. Mimi works at the United Nations. I had known her for a long time before I had any idea where she was from. Surely she could not have been born at the U.N.? I eventually found out that she was originally from Hong Kong; only a place like that has the ability to produce linguistic prodigies. Her parents are from Hubei province, so the Hubei dialect is her native tongue. Beyond that, she knows Cantonese, Mandarin, and a "smidgen" of Shanghainese. She has been a simultaneous interpreter at the U.N. for a number of years, and aside from English and French, she also knows Spanish, Russian and Italian. Whenever I think of this I start to lose it: I have been studying English for twenty years, and I'm still only at a junior high school level.

Mimi's other guest is up as well. Dima, a Muscovite working temporarily as a translator at the U.N., has made his quota of American dollars and is now shopping madly before returning home for Christmas. Mimi's apartment has become a free international hotel, putting up people from all over the globe. It serves Chinese food, French wine, and is without any language barriers. What more could one ask?

A shaft of light pokes its way between the buildings and shines in through the floor-to-ceiling window, refracting its glare off the grand piano. A traditional English breakfast: fried tomatoes and smoked salmon, along with fresh fruit. Dima and I sit down with Mimi between us, seeming a bit like a working breakfast of the leaders of superpowers. Dima expresses his frustration with the contrast between his national self-respect and the power of the American dollar, and I convey my understanding. He agrees with my critique of American foreign policy, and invites me to visit him in Moscow when I have time. I willingly accept his invitation, but due to a few technical problems, I am not able to reciprocate and invite him to Beijing.

Dima leaves to go shopping and Mimi heads off to work at the U.N.; Fifi is lively for a few minutes, then sighs and splays herself out in the doorway.

I give Mr. A a call on the phone. I have known him for twenty years. His life has been like some unfinished tale of adventure with an extremely convoluted plot that's always ready to take a new twist. At thirteen he was declared a reactionary and tried to drown himself, but he was rescued. He was then sent into exile along with his father to the far Northwest. When the Cultural Revolution came he was again pronounced a reactionary, but this time he didn't try to drown himself; instead taking flight. He wandered to every corner, and was eventually reduced to begging for food. In the 1970s he returned to

Beijing where we worked together — he as an art editor. After June Fourth he took refuge abroad, first working as a Fengshui master, and later as a military analyst.

"I just can't sleep lately," sighed Mr. A. "Think about it: I've been working on this for almost two years, and how could I not be worried? Lee Teng-hui is out of his mind, not stupid, just out of his mind. If Taiwan goes independent, the mainland won't simply stand by and watch, and then the United States will get involved. The Young Turks in the military are advocating war. The first target of that nuclear submarine in the Pacific is New York, which is to say, my home. What do you think I should do? I've just bought a house, should I move? And if war breaks out there won't be just one bomb, but several hundred at the least. Where is there to move to?"

I had heard that his predictions concerning these final series of events in the Taiwan Straits had been acknowledged as valid by the Pentagon and the Japanese Self-Defence Force.

After hanging up the phone, the scenario for the end of the world that Mr. A had outlined made breakfast hard to digest. He had, unfortunately, been correct in his prediction of the June Fourth repression, although he had been off by seven or eight years. At 2:30 in the afternoon Eliot Weinberger arrives. Before the world comes to an end, we still have to give a reading.

We go downstairs to Third Avenue and walk the four blocks to Grand Central, where we take the R train to Queens. All my memories of New York are suffused with the odor of urine in the subways. I chat with Eliot on the way there. He talks about people taking stimulants every day, and how the president of Mexico has sent military officers to care for the critically ill Octavio Paz, that the best part of New York is watching the passersby on the street, that Reagan has destroyed the American welfare system, Iceland is a paradise, Nina has gone to India on business, leaving him to get the kids off to school every day . . . we arrive at the station and take a taxi to Queens College.

Today is the 23rd of February 1998, and I am sitting in front of the computer trying to describe a day I spent in New York two months ago. Trying to reconstruct time is an absurd project, particularly in regard to the details that give time its shape; they have long since vanished. What are regarded as facts are simply contemporary supposition, with a bit of conspiracy thrown in.

So, I call up Mimi and Eliot, as if we were all criminals trying to get our alibis straight: "What did we have for breakfast that day?" "No, it wasn't Russian food." "What was the name of that professor?" Right, his name was Ammiel Alealy.

The campus is made up of a group of Spanish-style brick buildings. Several young female students stand smoking lazily at the gate, with that New York attitude of world-weary indifference. Professor Alealy suddenly appears, cutting across a little path, as if he had been hiding all along in the corner of a building. His face looks like a rough sketch done quickly, with a graying beard and quizzical eyes that clearly show a lack of sleep. His office is covered in drawings, some by his children, others by his students. He appears to favor the visual arts, and is a ready subject — some teachers are simply made to be drawn by their students.

He and Eliot had been neighbors for many years, and the nostalgic conversation of old neighbors commences as it does the world over. Translated into the Beijing dialect, it would run something like this: Remember that little three-roomed place by the coal-bin? Tore it down and built a new hotel, blocks out the sun completely. And those three girls you had your eye on? Getting a bit long in the tooth by now. How about the old man in the courtyard to the east? I'd call him lucky: not a cough or a gasp, just went to sleep one night and never woke up . . . .

Only about twenty people come to the reading, and most of these probably have been forced by the school, or are here for the free wine at the reception. The president of the college is anchoring the proceedings, which keeps anyone from daring to slip out. I read the poems in Chinese and Eliot reads his English translations. The twenty people in the audience are like twenty computers hooked up to the internet who have had their power cut off — all sent messages are simply bounced back. I exchange glances with Eliot, and we wind things up as fast as we can.

Professor Alealy represents the college at dinner, accompanied by four of my compatriots. We all follow on his heels as he looks for his car. At first he is confident of the direction, but after he has taken a hundred or so steps he becomes a bit hesitant, craning his head first front, then back. He eventually finds the car, but has lost the key. He searches his pockets, pauses to reflect, then begins to circle the vehicle like an amateur car thief. It starts to rain and Eliot and I retreat under the eaves of a nearby building. The professor is beginning to look more miserable, but there is nothing to do but take a taxi.

Once we are seated at the Chinese restaurant, Alealy is comforted by the food and calms down considerably, the lines on his face smoothing out into a more positive demeanor. The key to his car is destined to await him in some secret location. He is the sort of teacher that would attract the interest of the FBI. He is Jewish, yet sides with the Palestinians. His literary taste also runs outside the mainstream, as he studies Serbian poetry and has edited an anthology of Palestinian literature.

Eliot tells me that, in addition to the major Western languages, he knows Serbian, Greek, Hebrew and Arabic. Lost as he is in the labyrinth of all these ancient languages, it is no wonder that he can't find his keys.

I have an appointment with Susan Sontag at nine, so I rush from the restaurant to her place, arriving a good forty minutes late. She had actually asked me out for dinner, something I had completely forgotten.

You've eaten? There was a look of amazement in her eyes.
I've eaten. Some relationships are bound to run at cross-pur-
poses. Last year at a reception at the American PEN Center
she became the center of attention as soon as she walked in the
door, flashbulbs following the streaks of white in her black
hair. At dinner she had come over and introduced herself,
wanting to arrange a time for us to meet. I panicked and quickly
came up with an excuse. Later I sent her one of my books to
make up for it, but she never received it, something that can
only be attributed to fate.

Susan has a large penthouse apartment; the Hudson River
is visible from the living room. A tour boat floats by, clarifying
one's perception of the river in the dark of night. She tells me
that she likes to write in the kitchen.

Susan is not as self-important as legend would have it. She
opens a bottle of red wine and we begin to chat, and as with a
number of other Western writers, there appears the same deli-
cate psychological problem: the embarrassment of a writer at a
loss for words. With my level of English, what sort of conver-
sation can I really have with people?

When I get up to go, I am a bit unsteady from the wine.
Susan asks me to give a misdelivered package to the doorman.
I turn the matter over in my mind and finally decide that I am
up to the task.

I flag a cab. The driver is Turkish, and exclaims all the way
home: " . . . This world is done for. Haven't you heard? The

fucking polar ice caps are melting. Ha, Ha! The waters are rising and pretty soon Russia and Europe are going to be flooded." As he says this he takes a flat glass bottle and pours the contents into his mouth.

"Where are you from? China? China won't escape either, nor will our Turkey; we're all going to feed the fishes. God? God won't do anything. But don't worry, New York will go first. Ha, Ha! . . . all these big buildings will soon be at the bottom of the sea . . . . "

MOVING

In the six years between 1989 and 1995, I lived in seven different countries and moved fifteen times. I have to admit that this behavior verges on the insane, and that I moved so often I almost left the whole category of nation behind. When I think about it carefully, I realize that aside from external compulsion, there must be an even deeper impulse at work. I am fond of the words of the Peruvian poet César Vallejo: "You float nothingly behind . . ."

West Berlin was my first stop. My place there was near the affluent Kurfurstendam, provided by the German institute for academic exchange (DAAD). June Fourth had been a kind of high fever and I passed in front of the memorial church in a daze, shutting out all the exterior clamor. A punk with a blood-red Mohawk opened his mouth, but no sound emerged. The wall was still up that summer, cutting Berlin off from the world like a deserted island. I am the 1989 version of Robinson Crusoe, having just abandoned a sinking ship with my empty suitcase, digging my way into the dense grammatical thickets of the German language jungle. I hung the hammock I had bought in Mexico on the balcony and lay there gazing at the rocking sky. I had barely left when Berlin's wall came crashing down after me.

I then moved to Oslo, where I lived in the University area. I would occasionally walk to the center of town, the peaceful harbor providing a complete contrast with my turbulent interior. It was not until then that I realized there would be no going home.

I had been there hardly two days when Chen Maiping drove his ancient Mercedes over to help me move to yet another student dorm. By now I had two suitcases, but even so there was no way I could stuff my hammock into either one, so I filled it full of kitchen utensils and dragged it along to my new place. I shared a kitchen with five Norwegian guys. The only problem with that arrangement was that of the six bottles of beer I'd put in the refrigerator, four and a half immediately disappeared. Beer was extremely expensive in Norway. I slammed back the remaining half and took the last bottle back to my room.

My second experience with Norwegian beer came when I took Duo Duo to visit a professor, and the host entertained us with a home brew. The beer had an odd, soapy taste and we had not drunk very much before the two of us sank into sleep. The professor was angry enough to call all his friends: "my, my Chinese guests both fell asleep . . . ."

When winter arrived, Northern Europe showed me its true color: inky-black. A Chinese student of mine, who specialized in selling used televisions, took pity on me and found a set. I sat in front of the TV drinking warm beer until Norwegian became familiar to me, sounding a bit like the North Shanxi accent.

Having spent so much time in Norway, Maiping seemed to have become aphasic. The two of us made dinner every night, and the four of us — counting our shadows — sat there mute. During the winter break he went away to visit his wife. The University area emptied out, and I wandered around like an abandoned spirit. One evening I popped into a Chinese restaurant in which there was only one other customer. He was talking to himself and making odd movements; his eyes had an insane glint to them that was powerfully suggestive. In a panic, I put down my chopsticks and ran.

After New Year 1990, I gave my hammock to Maiping for him to use as a fishing net and moved to Stockholm, where I lived in a very spacious apartment. The owner and his family were visiting India. I actually used only the kitchen, but would loiter in the living room and dining room just long enough to take care of the houseplants. A group of Chinese exiles from a refugee camp in another country came to stay, each one of them bringing his or her own story of flight. Among them were workers, businessmen and university students, all of whom had come to the ends of the earth to pursue a course in loneliness. We borrowed light from each other while we lived in the winter darkness.

The winter in Stockholm is profoundly depressing: the sun no sooner comes up, hardly rising much at all before it is once again devoured by the leviathan, emitting a faint few bubbles in the form of lamplight. I barely got out of bed day or night, and never even bothered to open the curtains. Three months later, with the natural world yet to return to life, the owners returned from India. A well-meaning Chinese restaurateur then provided a small apartment for me. Its tiny size fit better with my sense of isolation. Someone brought back a bottle of whiskey from England, and I drank it in one sitting. I locked myself in my room and let out a sharp scream, terrifying myself when I looked up into the mirror.

I often went out drinking with Li Li, who wrote poetry in Swedish and had published a number of books. An inveterate womanizer, he flirted with all of the girls whenever he went out. In Stockholm nearly every bar has a gaming table. When we had lost all our spare cash and had drunk ourselves into a near stupor, we would stagger down the street and Li Li would suddenly begin to laugh hysterically.

Summer followed spring and I still kept the windows closed, now to shut out the loud brightness of night.

That autumn I moved to Aarhus — Denmark's second city — to teach, and ended up staying for two years. Anne Wedell-Wedellsberg found me a wing in a nice little house in the suburbs. The two landladies were both staunch feminists, one a psychologist and the other the curator of a woman's museum.

They each had a baby and lived in the main part of the house, from which they obtained a commanding view of the oriental male down on his luck. In the small hours of the night, three androgynous lamps reflected their solitary light onto one another. The little yard verged on the railroad tracks, and trains often intruded into my dreams. I would wake up with a start and, staring at the light sweeping across the wall, not know where I was.

My parents brought my daughter to visit. I decided for the moment to try to be a bit more decorous, so I moved into a building next to an admiral in the Danish navy. We lived on the second floor; outside was the sea and the Danish flag. On the first floor lived Olaf, an old architect, and Ola, a young pianist, rented the basement. Olaf lived by himself and had the confidence of an old bachelor; all he needed to enjoy classical music was a hand-held transistor radio.

I occasionally visited him for a drink. He admired I.M. Pei to no end, and since I am also Chinese, some of that esteem rubbed off on me. Building houses, however, provides people with places to live, while poets only construct paper houses, which actually give people the feeling of being homeless. When it came my turn to mow the lawn, Olaf put on a stern face and obliged me to push the lawn mower around the back yard.

Ola was single and lived on her teaching and work as an accompanist. She held a vague expression in her eyes, as if she had been staring too long at the sea. She was envious of my frequent trips to other places, and dreamt of finding work in a big city like Paris or New York. She really did play the piano well, but her sound was always completely blocked out by the closed door.

When my parents and daughter left, I moved to a new area in the suburbs in an effort to economize. The absentee landlords were an old Chinese couple who had fled along with their son after June Fourth and were enjoying the benefits of the Danish welfare state.

It was a peculiar unit, as the bathroom opened up into the center, and all the rooms surrounding it opened into one another. When I was in a good mood, I wandered around clockwise; if not, counter-clockwise. This was probably why the architect had taken such pains to design the place in this exact way, knowing that caged animals and convicts let out for exercise will always walk in a circle.

In early October of 1992, I moved from Denmark to Holland. I sent on what I could, and threw away more, but in the end I was still left sitting anxiously among a heap of luggage. There was nothing for me to do but to ask my friend from Berlin for help. He rented a van in Berlin, drove it to Denmark, packed it full of the possessions of my solitary self, and drove through Germany to Leiden.

My place in Leiden was much too small to allow me to wander, so I simply became another piece of the aged furniture. Maria, the widowed, neurotic landlady lived on the second floor. She had a son who seldom showed his face. Every year she went to a convent to take a psychological cure. This old woman, clearly on the verge of madness, grasped at the straws of my personal life and commenced talking without end about anything at all. I did my best to avoid her. Maria had the uncanny ability to detect the opening of my door, even if it was only a crack; she would stand there waiting, singing a French song, reciting a German poem, or retelling me the content of her nightmares. No matter what, I never let her into my room, as then she would become my nightmare.

Maria was tight with her money. In the frigid winters I wrote at night; she shut off the heat at midnight. I made a request for more heat the next morning, but she ignored me. After shivering for three more days, I made yet another request, and this time she granted a special dispensation. She reset the time for 2 a.m.— the hour directly between fervent hopes and nightmares.

I invited Maria out to eat at a neighborhood Chinese restaurant. She carefully made herself up and sat there waiting for me for some time. No one had probably asked her out to eat for a while. There weren't many people in the restaurant and Maria seemed somewhat uneasy, saying very little. She talked about Holland during the war and about her youth. On the way home her high heels tapped the road in the night with no wind.

Just before I left Leiden she asked me upstairs for tea, and I left a forwarding address. Her letters chased me all over, and though I moved about quite rapidly, they caught up to me every time. With each letter she enclosed a self-addressed envelope, but I hardened my heart and threw them all away. In this world no one can save anyone else, my lonely Maria!

II

I stayed in Paris for three months before I came to the United States. I first found lodging at the home of my French translator, Chantal Chen. She is divorced with two children, and lives in a small town on the edge of Paris. She built the house herself, and it will never be completed. Every time I go to Paris she points out the changes: a new bathroom here, a hole that has just been poked in the ceiling there.

She is fond of ranting about life, and she doesn't stop at mere ranting, instead bravely vacillating between realism and nihilism: teaching, cooking, translating, mowing the lawn. Sometimes I worry what would happen if she confused them. Would she cook her writings, or mow my poems? She loves ballet, something that without a doubt effectively inhibits confusion. I have never seen her dance, but I can imagine her in the practice room: taking a deep breath, standing on her toes, spreading her arms, twirling, maintaining her balance . . . .

My parents came with my daughter to Paris. Song Lin and his family were away on vacation and left their key for us. Their apartment was on the fifth floor in the center of town. The winding staircase creaked like a wounded spine into the Parisian night. My mother has bad legs, so climbing stairs is painful for her. These stairs reminded me of my recurring nightmare — the one where I'm climbing an endless staircase.

Paris in summer belongs to foreigners, and nearly every day I took my daughter to the playground in the park. I would take a book along and soak up the sun while sitting on a bench, my heart softening to the point that tears came readily. I felt like a sentimental old man. The book would slide off and I would fall asleep in the sunlight until my daughter woke me.

My three months in Paris seemed like the run-up to a long-jump: I put down my burdens, loaded up on Bordeaux wines, tensed all my muscles, and let myself leap.

On August 25, 1993, I carried through customs and immigration a passport endorsed with an intent to immigrate, and landed my dusty self in the new world, with absolutely none of the panache that Columbus had brought with him back then. I ended up first in Ypsilanti, Michigan. Larry, my first American landlord, greeted me with a shrewd smile. He was an electrician at the University of Michigan, a city councilman, a Democrat, a divorced man living by himself, a father of two children, and the owner of a cat. When he was not busy wooing voters he was taking part in a singles club — moving busily between politics and sex. He was correct about one thing: politics as public sex, and sex as private politics.

Larry was seldom at home, so I often sat on his front porch and read. I was taking a course on the novel at Eastern Michigan University, and every week we had to read at least one experimental novel in English. My English was pretty bad, so I had to struggle hopelessly with everything that I had forgotten at my age. I read until I became so frustrated that I couldn't go on, at which point I began to appraise the passing pedestrians. It was the height of autumn, and golden leaves covered both the sky and earth. At night the students would drink and talk loudly in exaggerated phrases. Their youthful despair had become no more than a distant echo of my own experiences.

Larry had an ugly yellow cat, with dirty fur and a furtive expression — in this respect very much like Larry. It openly ignored me, not even trying to get me to feed it when it was hungry, something quite contrary to the basic nature of cats. Owing to my drifter's sensitivity, I became certain that this behavior was the result of Larry's surreptitious instruction. During the day a black cat would appear at the window, observing the actions of Larry's cat. Because the house protected him, however, the yellow cat paid no attention to him. The two cats confronted one another, and time passed as slowly as their movements.

One day I carried the yellow cat out the back door and the black cat sidled over, growling sonorously from a place deep in his white belly. The fur on Larry's cat stood on end as it scuttled under the back stairs, preparing to fight to the death. While the black cat had the advantage, it did not venture any rash moves. From that point on, the yellow cat was aware of my wicked intentions and ceased his disrespect, giving me as wide a berth as possible.

At the beginning of 1994, I moved to Ann Arbor. Since I couldn't drive, I found a place near the shopping district. While the brick bungalow was exceedingly ugly, it formed the perfect complement to the fast food restaurants, gas stations and traffic lights that made up the modern scenery in which it was set. For the first time I had the feeling of settling into a home, so I wasted a week buying furniture, electrical appliances and ordinary household items. I even bought a little pot of ivy. Owing to the interpretive power of these various goods, the concept of "home" finally took on some meaning. When I had everything arranged I wandered about my house like a thief, but quite self-satisfied.

I quickly grew weary of the monotonous scenery and neighbors, and I was still excited by the idea of travel. Whenever I take a train or plane, I am gripped by a peculiar excitement. An American girl told me once that airports were the places she most preferred, as she loved the atmosphere. Actually, traveling is a form of living, and a traveler's life is always situated between departure and arrival. It makes no difference where one is coming from or going to; what is important is to preserve a sense of the unknown and to take oneself in hand in one's wanderings, yes, *float nothingly*.

I became infatuated with jazz, and wanted to move back to an America of an earlier time. Xu Yong helped me read through the want ads, make phone calls and visit houses, until we finally found something. The little street was quiet and out of the way, if a bit desolate. Most of the two-story wood frame houses had been built in the 1920s and, what with their peeling paint, had a dejected feel. But they perfectly evoked the spirit I was searching for. Many people went to see the house that evening and those who were interested arranged themselves in order of their arrival. I was fifth in line, but the four ahead of me could not make up their minds, so I got the house.

Much of the time writing simply provided an excuse for me to sit in front of the window and stare into space. A squirrel ran across the telephone wires, balancing itself with its bushy tail. A persimmon tree in the distance burned with fruit. There was a glider on the front porch, the iron chains of which squeaked whenever you sat on it.

I lived on the second floor and the old landlady lived on the first. We had never met. On the days the trash was collected, piles of paper food containers appeared at her door. One day while I was dawdling on the glider, I saw a side door push open and a cane poke its way out and hook onto the newspaper lying on the ground. I quickly bent down and handed it to her. The landlady was extremely old, probably over ninety, and she spoke exceedingly slowly, the words being pulled out of her like so much taffy. I suddenly had an image of her sitting on the glider when she was young.

Her son, who was a laywer, told me she had suffered several strokes that had put her in the hospital many times, but she was bound and determined not to move, not to leave the house she had lived in since the day she had gotten married. As someone who had become accustomed to moving, I expressed my admiration for this sense of purpose. The massive house of her son was located deep in the woods. His wife was an extremely pleasant person, who always let me sample her freshly baked cookies. They owned numerous properties that they rented out, but insisted on mowing each lawn themselves. Every weekend the couple would be busy, wearing straw hats, putting out snacks, sweating profusely, and all for what? I never did understand their enthusiasm for hard labor.

In the autumn of 1995, my family reunited in a small town in Northern California where we settled down, first in an apartment and later in a house that we bought. I would sometimes sit in the back yard and wonder if I hadn't been the stationary one over the past few years, while the greater world arena had been the thing in motion.

I recalled Maria, who, playing her solitary part upon this stage, grasped at her letters with their indistinct addresses until they were blown away by the cold wind, vanishing into the air. For the first time I thought of writing back to her: Dear Maria, I'm doing all right. And you?

DRIVING

My car broke down and sat by the side of the road shoot-
ing out steam. A friend of mine who knows cars took a look
and decided that the radiator had sprung a leak, and found
someone to come and fix it. I'd bought the car last year, an '86
Audi. At the time I was actually looking for a car for someone
else, but as soon as I set my eyes on this one, I wanted it for
myself. Its opulent aura mimicked a stern German arrogance,
and under the streetlights, it looked almost perfect. What par-
ticularly enticed me was sitting back in the leather seat listen-
ing to the CD player, its ten speakers surrounding me like so

many angels in heaven. I thought to myself that even if the car didn't run, it would still be worth it to have it sitting in front of the house, serving as both study and music room.

Its steering wheel, however, did have a problem: you had to continually turn to the left in order to get the car to move straight ahead — in this respect it was a bit like the thought processes of certain rulers. The owner was an American, whose casual manner did not inspire quick confidence, but the price was amazingly low: $2,650. And for someone as addicted to good sound systems as I am, I didn't have the heart to bargain, so we struck a deal at $2,600. The vehicle's flaws were readily apparent the next morning when the sun came out. Aside from the problem with the steering wheel, there was damage to the body, the leather seats were worn, and I couldn't close the sun roof once I'd opened it. When I got the car back from the garage its price had doubled.

I am probably like any number of men from mainland China with my love for speed. And this probably stems from the youthful fantasies we had growing up in an agricultural empire. In the early 1970s, the American bestseller *Jonathan Livingston Seagull* captivated a good number of people when it was translated into Chinese; my brother, for instance, copied the whole thing out by hand. Whenever I am driving fast down an empty highway I think of this story, especially at dusk, and it makes me happy, especially with this sound system around me.

I refused to learn to drive for many years. The main reason being my serious neurasthenia, which puts me right to sleep whenever I ride in a car. This posed no problem in Europe, where the public transportation systems are well developed. But when I moved to the United States I began to fully experience the pain of having no car and constantly having to find transportation. At the time I was teaching extra classes at another university that was only seven miles from where I lived, but it took me several hours to get there through a combination of walking and the bus. I gritted my teeth and decided to buy an '86 Ford Tempo. I spotted it in the classified ads of the newspaper, and its price, mileage and age all seemed about right. I talked to the owner on the phone and a friend took me over to take a look at it.

The owner turned out to be student from mainland China. The car looked pretty old on the outside, and it was blind in one headlight, the result, the owner said, of a collision with a deer that was fatal to the latter. The original asking price was $1,950, but I bargained him down $300 and we both seemed relieved. We first took it to a garage to clean it up, and for a moment it actually seemed to sparkle. After that we went around to various wrecking yards in search of a headlight. Every morning after I got up I would go out to my aged car, polish it here, fix it there, and then walk around it a few times before I could bear to leave it.

Learning to drive is simply a matter of overcoming psychological obstacles. When one is older, reaction time slows down, not to mention my utter lack of a sense of direction. I did everything by the book, first practicing in a parking lot. I remember that the first time I drove on the street was at night; with headlights blazing and horn blaring, I panicked and the car began to pitch and roll as if it were on a stormy sea. I so terrified my friend in the passenger seat that he started screaming, and looked ready to throw himself from the car.

The local Chinese all go through the same drill, which makes driving school unnecessary. You can take the written exam in Chinese, but there are only three sets of questions, all of which have been lovingly passed down by generations of student drivers. So all you need to do is spend about two hours studying and you are guaranteed to pass. To avoid suspicion, however, one is advised to intentionally give a wrong answer or two. I was indiscreet and passed with no errors at all, at which point the examiner gave me a look and asked, "Have you ever driven before?" I flatly denied it. The examination course for the driving test is also set and hasn't been altered for at least ten years; it has become a conveyor belt delivering batch after batch of Chinese drivers onto the perilous highway network. A friend maneuvered me over the set course three times just before I took the exam. The examiner was a young attractive black woman, something that gave me pause, as pretty women are notorious sources of danger for me. After the exam was over, she pointed out that I had driven too slowly and cornered too fast. My heart sank at hearing this, and I was completely unprepared when she raised her delicately outlined eyebrows and said: "You pass."

Buying a used car is like buying heartache. The under-pan of my car was too low, and once when I was practicing my driving it scraped some rocks, becoming as unruly as a tank and discharging clouds of thick smoke. I immediately took it to the garage where I found out that the carburetor was busted. To replace it, parts and labor would be $500. After the carburetor was changed, the husky mechanic still would not shut up. He told me that the muffler and the whole exhaust system needed to be replaced, as the salt spread on the streets during the Midwestern winter had corroded it beyond repair. I gnashed my teeth and stomped around, but eventually had to admit that I was just plain out of luck. After the car was repaired, the mechanic wrote out sheet after sheet of bills, the combination of which added up to what I had paid for the car in the first place. As I drove my now unsputtering, but still dilapidated, car home, I hardly need mention the resentment I was feeling.

I suspect every student from mainland China has had this sort of unhappy experience. When you first get here, you are anxious to have a car to drive to work, but you have little money and you can't be too choosy. My friend Guo bought an old car for $200 when he got here ten years ago, and after practicing driving it for an hour and a half, he took it out onto the freeway. Just as he was beginning to feel pleased with himself, the brake pedal went out as he was going downhill, and all he could do was close his eyes as he ran into the rear end of a huge truck. Fortunately, no one was hurt, but the driver of the truck came over, and discovering that Guo could not speak English, and that he was driving a wreck that should have long since been taken off the road, cursed him roundly before stalking off.

When I saw Guo two years later, he was still working, but he was a little better off. He had paid $435 for a Honda, which was in reasonably good shape, and had only a single flaw: it was very difficult to get it to turn over. In order to get it going he would have to park on a hill and use momentum, something that required real art.

During my visit, the job of starting the car was handed over to me. At first it worked pretty well, as I would only have to push it a little more than a hundred yards before it started to emit its cheery blue smoke. Each time, however, it got harder and the car occasionally failed to turn over even after pushing it for more than half a mile. Running through the wind and snow until my body was soaked with sweat definitely demanded my heroic revolutionary spirit.

When we were having dinner at his place before going to the airport, I begged him to keep the car running no matter what, otherwise I'd be sure to miss my flight.

In the United States, buying cars is a science. It is best first to seek the advice of experts and not rush in too boldly. There are car auctions that advertise themselves with a splash, but the cars on sale are all of suspect origins. They are nonetheless extremely cheap, and attract numerous students from mainland China. A car is driven once around a track and you raise your hand; if no one else outbids you, the car is yours. I know one young man from Nanjing who caught the buying fever and drove a car home from an auction. Everyone crowded around to inspect it, and couldn't figure out why it had been so cheap. Eventually understanding dawned — the car had no reverse.

After you've been in America long enough, buying a car is no big deal — sooner or later the novelty wears off. But remember the first time you legally sat behind the steering wheel, started the engine, put it into gear and touched the throttle? The car leaps forward, the scenery flashes by, and only red lights and the police can stop you.

GAMBLING

This Christmas the whole family went to Las Vegas. We started by driving to Los Angeles and spending the night there, then went skiing in the mountains the next morning. That afternoon we went down the other side of the mountains and entered a vast expanse of desert.

At night, after the sun has set, an endless line of headlights stretches along I-15 toward the gambling city. And today is Christmas day; what sinners they all must be.

GAMBLING

We arrive in Las Vegas at nine. The splendor of the city, built on human weakness, takes away your strength. Someone told me that in her later years Eileen Chang suddenly decided to move here. I can believe it. After reading her stories, it's easy to find many things within them that correspond to this city.

Passing through the main door, the temptations of the flesh assault you all at once. Fortunately I remain steadfast, and all it takes for me to get through is to feed a few coins into the slot machines. The rooms we had originally booked had been occupied, so we were given a free upgrade to a deluxe suite on the twenty-seventh floor. After dinner, my wife and daughter felt tired and decided to soak in the spa included in the room. I said I was going for some change and would be back shortly.

I have loved to gamble ever since I was young. My father smoked and I would take the empty packs of cigarettes and tear them into flat pieces, which I folded into a triangular shape with the edges pointing down slightly. We children would gather together and first identify those who were bringing damaged packs, or those of inferior brands, all of whom had to stand aside. To be able to flip the little triangles over took a good angle of attack and real finesse. But I was never very coordinated, so even when I jumped up as high as I could and fanned with all my strength, the flattened out cigarette packs refused to budge. And all my opponents had to do was shrug their shoulders and my packs flipped over and became theirs.

That kind of gambling was a sort of primitive exchange — goods bartered for other goods.

Later on I became infatuated with marbles. We would all bend over and move around behind five little holes in the ground. I still had my coordination problem, and the marbles I shot had neither aim nor force when they left my hand. Those with talent used a completely different stance: backs straight and even, taking aim with one eye cocked. Whenever I heard a sharp crack, my heart sank and I knew my marble had another chip in it. Those guys were merciless; they used marbles made of porcelain or even rock to chip my pure glass marbles. In junior high school we played marbles during recess and I invariably lost a white sheet of paper that was supposed to be used for math homework. When it came time for me to do my homework in the evening, I had to dash around trying to borrow another piece of paper.

During the hard years of the early 1960s, our neighbors distributed their rations evenly among the family. Xiaojing and his older brother each received 1,500 soybeans for the month. The two of them played marbles for the allotment, but Xiaojing's technique was inferior, and with every try he lost five more beans. One time he lost forty, almost enough for a full meal for his brother, but we urged him to bet another forty to make up the loss in one shot. They went again, and he instantly owed eighty. When the number he'd lost had reached 1,200, he suddenly pulled out a win and got them all back.

When I visited Shenzhen at the end of 1985 for a writers' conference, I encountered slot machines for the first time. Before I'd put in very many coins, I'd won: a bell rang and a pile of Hong Kong dollars began to tumble out. My fellow professionals were envious and started after the cascading coins, stealing as many as they could. We all carried a miniature roulette wheel into our next meeting, and literature took a downhill course thereafter.

In the spring of 1986, I sailed from Stockholm to Helsinki. There were slot machines all over the boat. In the second class cabin each porthole contained a bright sun sparkling on the sea, but I had an urgent desire to win some money, and had my eye out for the right slot. First I shook hands with it, then began my attack and before half an hour, two hundred Swedish kronor, enough to buy two hundred meat dumplings, had vanished without a trace. I took out my dinner money and continued my battle with the cannibalistic slot. Still doing well — it cleaned me out completely. The deck began to roll. My legs weakened and sparks appeared before my eyes —time to repent and give way? I suddenly remembered the thirty U.S. dollars I had exchanged before I left China. I got it, changed it, and continued to insert coins until I was staring at the machine as it consumed my last hard-earned krona. Since there was nobody around, I gave the machine a couple of good hard kicks. When I got back to my cabin it was already dark, and I was so hungry that I ate the rock-hard piece of complimentary chocolate that had been left there.

I spent a year in the north of England, from where I would occasionally visit London. The noise of the slot machine parlors there is deafening, a sound that got my blood racing even from a substantial distance. Those places seemed to be a giant funnel for all the world's money. There are many Asian faces within, all of which belong to the workers at London's Chinese restaurants. The owners and master cooks dare to enter into the great ocean of proper gambling, but the workers only stand on the shore skipping stones.

The nickname "one-armed bandit," is apt in their ability to murder and steal. Since I have been victimized many times before, I never dare spend much time with them. I generally try to limit myself to the twenty minutes or so before I am scheduled to meet someone, hoping to win a little something. Then, since my credibility and friendship are at stake, I have to quit and move on. Also, when playing the slots, one must watch out for their conspirators: once when I wasn't paying attention, a two-armed bandit was nimble enough to steal 180 pounds from me.

I met the Guo brothers in England. They originally played in an orchestra in China — one the Chinese flute and the other the Suona, a kind of Chinese bassoon. Playing these two instruments with their desolate sounds, they brought out emotions connected to weddings and funerals with them to London, where they managed to catch the attention of even the sophisticated English. The Guo brothers played on the streets for a living and were quite popular, but the money that they earned had to go somewhere. Both of them were gamblers.

Only those with a rich store of knowledge, vast experience and a life-long dedication are worthy of this appellation. It is not just for anyone. One night Guo the elder lost over a hundred pounds to the slots. He was reduced to ten pence, which he fed into the machine, only to have two pounds spit back. He put in some more and won four, then eight. Then he went into the casino and immediately won eighty pounds at roulette. He kept at it and couldn't seem to lose, eventually ending up with nine thousand pounds by dawn. When he gets this far in the story, Guo's eyes gleam bright and he sighs — one knows this must be the turning point. After having breakfast at the casino, he took a cab to a friend's house and asked him to wire two thousand pounds to his mother in Beijing as a filial contribution.

After that he went to the appliance store and bought a VCR. When he got home he took a hot bath and then returned to the casino, and to a reversal of fortune, gave back six thousand pounds right away. He then got in another cab and hurried back to his friend's house, learning that the two thousand pounds had not yet been sent.

Alas, before the old lady even heard a breath, the sum was gone in a puff of smoke. By evening he had given back all nine thousand pounds, plus another four thousand of his own.

Guo's wife is English and she went to the casino and made a scene. There was nothing the manager could do but strip Guo of his membership rights in the club.

It was 1988 when I was on the same program as the Guos in Manchester. My poetry reading attracted little attention but the Guos' playing moved the audience of expatriate Chinese to hot tears. After the show we found a little restaurant in Chinatown. When we had eaten and drunk our fill, Guo the elder told his story — that twenty-four hours in his life. Reaching the end, he still refused to concede defeat, adding brusquely: "I've got their friggin' system figured out. If I could only get my hands on another ten thousand pounds, I could win everything back." I thought that the owner of the casino would be delighted to hear this, as it is exactly this thirst for revenge that is the real secret of a casino's fortune.

When I returned to England some years later, I asked about the Guos, and heard that they were still busking on the streets. That twenty-four hours of pain and joy must make its contribution to those desolate Chinese folk songs, rendering them even more puzzling.

II

Actually there are many stories of Chinese gambling while abroad. Chinese like to gamble, something that I think is related to a national propensity for the irrational — a belief in fate rather than gods. Add to this the condition of being away from home, cultural barriers, and the wish not to get too obsessed with oneself. What else can one do? At least in a casino there are all sorts of people gathered for the same purpose. There also are no linguistic or cultural barriers — all you have to do is gesture and everybody understands. Moreover, gambling gives one hope, if nothing else; if you lose today there is always tomorrow. And if you get really lucky, then you can bask in it for the rest of your life.

In the summer of 1995, I hitched a ride from Paris to Germany to visit some friends. I got to know the driver, Zhao, who seemed a straight shooter. He had been studying at a German university when he got sick of it and took a job working in the freezer of a large meat company. The pay was good, but Germans didn't want to do the work, so they left it for the third-world brotherhood. From one perspective the work wasn't very hard: all you had to do was pick up a bill of lading, put on a jacket, go into the meat locker, and pick up the side of pork or five chickens or whatever and carry them out. But you had better not dawdle or you will end up frozen and undiscovered until the next time someone goes in to fill an order.

When work was over, Zhao would follow everyone else to a casino and observe how the system worked. The next day while working at the meat locker he thought over what he had observed until he had figured out the key to the roulette wheel.

During the time I was in Germany, Zhao quit his job at the meat locker and went to work at the gambling tables. The tables were a good deal warmer than the inside of a freezer, he didn't have to touch the carcasses of dead animals, and there were even people waiting on him. He was in good spirits every day when he returned, and would have dinner with us as soon as he had finished counting his marks. He analyzed the day's events, plotted out his graph, and summarized the trend; aside from a few isolated errors, everything happened as he predicted. It seemed clear that the most significant day in the history of human gambling was almost upon us and I warned him not to win too much each day lest the casino notice and put him on their black list. My anxiety was superfluous, as three weeks later Zhao was back at work in the meat locker, along with a new burden of debt.

In point of fact, casinos don't object to your winning. Ten years ago an old man hit the jackpot at an electronic slot machine and won 300,000 dollars. The employees at the casino came over to congratulate him and to write him out a check. The old man was so intoxicated by his victory that he refused the check, saying he wanted to keep on playing. Three days later he had not only lost the 300,000, but had a tax bill of twenty thousand that he could only pay by going home and selling personal property. This was the best possible advertisement for the casino, as the news immediately appeared in the local newspaper.

Luck at the gaming tables is as hard to grasp as is fate itself, something that even the casino management is obliged to believe. If the house loses at Blackjack several times in a row, they immediately change the dealer, which in reality is an attempt to change their luck. I believe that between people there are fields of energy that are either beneficial or injurious. Should the dealer be a woman of ferocious mien who shuffles the cards between a pair of powerful hands, then you're half beaten before you even start — you have no hope of winning. Men of too great an age have an aura of expertise about them that is even more formidable. I was playing Twenty-one in Reno once and had won several hands in a row when a new dealer came on board, a man so old even his eyebrows had gone white. Going strictly by age, he should have retired twenty years before, but he was the casino's ace in the hole. He had difficulty standing up and his hands trembled when he dealt. If I had twenty, he inevitably had twenty-one. I was a step or two slow in making my escape, and easy as that, the table was swept clean of the customers' money.

The casinos in Europe are more restrained. They are semi-concealed and even a bit aristocratic, refusing to engage in the business of rescuing the masses from their spiritual agony. In 1992, I went to the south of France and decided to visit Monte Carlo while I was there. I made the mistake of going into the casino, and what I mean by *mistake* is that I overestimated my own capacities.

I was treated as an honored guest, something I found frankly overwhelming. A doorman dressed like a general opened the door for me, I was led in by an elderly man with white hair, and the young ladies had on their standard smiles. At the registration desk I handed over my passport and a fifty-franc registration fee and was duly entered in their database. I walked into the palatial main room by rounding a huge pillar; I looked all around and saw a few roulette tables; there was not a slot machine to be seen anywhere. There were not many people inside, and they all seemed to be regulars. They were immaculately dressed and talked in subdued tones. I approached one of the tables thinking I would try my luck, but I immediately noticed a discreet sign: 500 franc minimum bet. I only had 350, not even enough to purchase a single chip. A woman put down her bet — three million in franc chips. I broke into a slight sweat, stepped back and lit a cigarette. At that moment the camera was perhaps directly focused on me, and the attached computer was contacting Interpol and major banks trying to ferret out information about this Chinese tycoon.

The atmosphere in an American casino is completely different. The first time I went to Atlantic City I was astonished. It seemed to be the sacrificial altar of the future: hundreds of slot machines flashing their lights and emitting sounds, the people, as if put under a spell, with their mechanical movements and glazed eyes. It was a mass religious activity. When we got tired, we stepped outside for some air, but the only

thing visible was a huge pedestrian walkway suspended over-
head that stretched from the casino all the way to the sea-
shore. It scooped up all the stragglers and deserters, including
us, and siphoned us all back to the action.

Just now, as I'm descending from the twenty-seventh floor
penthouse to the lobby, the magic is calling to me. I begin by
exchanging twenty dollars for coins and commence my drill
with the one-armed bandit. Amidst the tumult I try my luck
more than a hundred times, and am clearly not making a go of
it. One time, when the change cart is nowhere to be seen, I
even insert bills directly into the slot in order to make change.
But heaven helps those who help themselves, and I eventually
win one; the bells go off and the machine spits out coins, not
stopping until four hundred have poured out. I look around,
trying to get the other patrons to share my good fortune, but
they react sluggishly and look my way without seeming to
really see anything. At best I get a curt nod; these people obvi-
ously know nothing of the world.

I put all my coins into a little bucket and am preparing to
take my leave when a scantily clad female attendant brings me
a drink. I tip her and take another. With the liquor now eking
out my courage, I can't stop. It is the pit of night, but there are
still a number of lost souls abroad, most of whom seem to be
Chinese; the sounds of my native tongue drift about me —
now near, now far. When I look up again, the room appears to
be obscured by fog, but this can't be, and must simply be the

result of the trance I am in. Opposite me an American woman wins and glances around in self-satisfaction. I understand, and hastily wave my hand in congratulations.

At about six in the morning I insert my last coin into the machine and make my way across the lobby, immediately getting lost. I have to ask an attendant the way to the elevators. With the ring of a bell, the door closes and the elevator rises toward the penthouse.

RECITING

When I was in primary school I was known for my ability at comic dialogue, but I later switched to dramatic reading, reciting Gao Shiqi's poem "The Song of the Times." I can remember the athletic field enveloped in dust, with the entire student body gathered around and the teachers supervising. I stood on the brick platform, raising my voice: *Oh time —* time, which sweeps by.

The Cultural Revolution can be thought of as a mass recitation led by Mao Zedong. Those at the back inevitably lost track of what was being said and ended up chanting counterrevolutionary slogans.

Moreover, there was an obvious problem with the pronunciation used on the Central Broadcasting Network: it made it seem as if the whole country was correcting the old man's high pitched Hunan accent word by word. I did odd jobs for our school's propaganda team. It was more interesting working backstage; almost metaphoric. And as metaphors are always slippery, and can be neither touched nor seen directly, they provide the ultimate interpretation. When the performance was concluded, and the recitations were finished, it was time for the metaphors to come along and confer meaning.

Mao eventually grew a bit world-weary and sought peace and quiet, thus shooing off all the young people to the factories, mines, and the countryside. I became a construction worker but I couldn't help breaking into song from time to time while on the job site. In the evening, those of us who shared this predilection climbed up on the roof and sang Chairman Mao's poems to the stars and to the assembled loudspeakers. We would also recite He Jingzhi's "Song of Lei Feng": *This is the way people should go, this is the road we should take!* The older workers all thought we were a bit touched in the head: "These young guys have been driven nuts by their inability to find a wife. No doubt about it."

In the spring of 1970, I went rowing with Yifan and Kangcheng on the lake at the Summer Palace. Kangcheng stood in the prow of the boat and declaimed:

My life is a whirling and dried up leaf,/ My future is a stalk of barley that will never ripen,/ If this is to be my true fate,/ I would as soon make a song to the wild thorns..."

I was extremely moved by the poem; Guo Lusheng's expression of perplexity.

Nine years later I met Guo. Everyone said he had gone mad, but it did not seem so to me. The only evidence for this was that he constantly shuttled back and forth between his home and a mental hospital. When he was with friends, he would suddenly venture the question: "May I recite a poem for everyone?" If no one demurred he would stand up, straighten his faded uniform and say, "Please let me know your frank opinion." He would maneuver his false teeth into place with his tongue and clear his throat. When he had finished one, he would smile modestly, "May I recite another?" Although his voice certainly had a cadence to it, he was actually quite restrained — very different from our way of declaiming revolutionary texts in those years.

What I refer to as our manner of revolutionary declamation was actually a combination of slaughterhouse squeals, as if one was receiving a sizeable electric shock. If the ordinary way of reciting poetry in those years were ever used today, people would almost certainly consider the speaker to be insane. From this perspective it was Guo Lusheng who was normal, and we and the epoch the ones gone mad.

On April 8th, 1979, the editorial board of *Today* organized a poetry reading at Yuyuantan park. We applied for permission to the police and received no response, which we took as tacit approval. I went with Mang Ke and Lao E to survey the terrain. There was a little clearing in the woods and a hill that could serve as our stage. Huang Rui painted an abstract pattern on a bed-sheet and hung it between two trees as our curtain. Lao E went out to round up some storage batteries so we could have an amplifier and some speakers. He looked a bit as if he were planning to make a homemade bomb. It was, in fact, an explosive device, which blew open a sizable breach: this was the first such privately organized poetry reading since 1949. It was very windy that day, which held the crowd down to four or five hundred, fewer than we'd expected. An aerial view would have revealed three distinct rings of color: the audience at the center dressed in gray and blue and khaki; then the foreigners in their garish clothes; finally the ring of police, all in white.

Chen Kaige, who was then still a student at the Cinema Institute, took part in the reading. He read Guo Lusheng's "Believing in the Future" and my "The Answer" that day, using the revolutionary mode of declamation. But the sculptor Wang Keping did just the opposite, reading Mang Ke's "October Offering" in a flat voice, as if he were talking to himself.

In the fall of 1984, *The Star* poetry magazine held "The Star Poetry Festival" in Chengdu, and I gained first-hand experience of the lunacy of people from Sichuan. Even before the event began, two thousand tickets had been snapped up. On the opening day a group of workers had volunteered to serve as security and maintain order, but people without tickets still poured in through the windows, throwing the place into chaos. The audience rushed the stage seeking autographs and ended up stabbing the poets with their fountain pens.

Gu Cheng, his wife, and I took refuge in the dressing room, dimmed the lights, and hid under a table. We heard heavy footsteps; people pushed open the door and rushed into the room, asking, "Where are Gu Cheng and Bei Dao?" We pointed in the other direction, "They slipped out the back door."

Ye Wenfu, who had been criticized for his poetry of political satire, received a hero's welcome. As he recited in his revolutionary cadence, someone shouted out: "Long live Ye Wenfu!" I figured that all he had to do was say the word and the audience would charge right out into the street behind him. When we got back to the hotel a group of young women circled around him massaging his back, reminding me of nothing so much as Mao Zedong in his later years. Sometimes everything is only a question of the correct verb tense: the young Mao Zedong was also Ye Wenfu.

Unfortunately, I did not enjoy this kind of good fortune, and the only person pursuing me was a young man from Dalian who had quit his job to become a wanderer; in his eyes I could see the fanaticism engendered by the crisscross of paths that lay before him. He followed me day after day, pouring forth his inner pain. I told him I understood, but asked if he might give it a rest for awhile. He said nothing more, instead pulling out a knife and stabbing himself in the palm, splashing blood all around. He then turned on his heels and left.

All this stemmed from a peculiar juncture of time — the blank period between the collapse of ideology and the advent of the tide of commercialism. Poets had put on a series of false masks: those of savior, warrior, pastor, rock star, all of which were reflected in a strange mirror compounded of extreme pressure and high temperature. And we came close to mistaking those images for our true selves. Very shortly, however, we were to be inundated in the commercial tide, which swept away the masks, shattered the mirrors, and insured that this mistake would never happen again.

In the summer of 1985, I left China for the first time. The Rotterdam poetry festival seemed something like a sect of a pagan religion, but even so it had nothing of the fanaticism I had seen in Chengdu. The audience was all well behaved, and nobody brought knives with which to dignify themselves through the person of the poet. They bought their programs or collections of poetry and kept to themselves; they applauded at the appropriate times; there was no shouting of slogans like "long live so-and-so." The audience is a lie detector that the poet must pass — don't even think about trying to intimidate it. And do not try to take over the stage, either, as the time for each individual reading is carefully scheduled. I figure that they are prepared to shut off the mikes if need be, to render mute any poets who might have a tendency to the hysterical. All in all it is run with characteristic capitalist precision.

Many poets are at odds with society, have scanty survival skills, and cannot escape the taint of unemployment, poverty or insanity; they are considered a breed apart. So, regardless of what other purpose they serve, poetry readings provide poets with the proof that they are neither deaf nor dumb, with a bit of free travel and the chance to become known to the rest of the world.

Actually, the experience of this type of event varies along with different national characteristics. The Barcelona poetry festival is run in a bold and unrestrained manner, like a carnival whose main intent is to extol time, good wine and love. As far as the Spaniards seemed to be concerned, enjoying life comes first. The daily activities concluded at 11 p.m., just when the locals sit down to dinner. When inspiration strikes, the poets puff up their chests, suck up their bellies, and make a grand progress to the waterfront. Waiters hover near, candlelight is reflected in the wineglasses, and gypsies sing and dance. After several glasses of wine, the gloom of a poet's life in the workaday world can be completely cast aside.

II

Poetry reading also has its perils. In the spring of 1993, I was part of a literary tour organized by the British Arts Council that included a visit to Belfast, a city in a state of war. The IRA would notify the authorities ten minutes before one of their bombings, to avoid harming their own people. We stayed at the Europa Hotel, which inspected everyone who entered (a year later I saw on television that it had been reduced to rubble). As our hostess walked us to a restaurant, she looked at her watch and announced that there would be a bomb going off in the vicinity in the next several minutes. I was about to take cover when I noticed the hostess's casual manner and decided just to stick close by her instead.

My translator, Wang Tao, and I went into a cinema playing *Patriot Games*, in which there was a total of only four or five viewers. When the film started the two of us were stunned to discover that it was an anti-IRA piece. Wasn't it absurdly risky to play this kind of trick on their home ground? Both of us instinctively ducked down with only our eyes showing, as if we were in a battlefield trench; we were intent upon avoiding any explosions, on-screen or off. It was the most thrilling movie I have ever seen in my life.

The reading was in a small theater that was surrounded by troops patrolling with automatic weapons. The audience consisted mostly of young people, and was mixed, with all political persuasions seemingly represented. When the readings began, everyone was fully absorbed, as if they had forgotten the war going on all around them. My own voice was oddly different that night, but not strictly out of fear. In a place like that, poetry actually matters.

There was, however, an even more perilous occasion. In the summer of 1992, Anne Wedell-Wedellsberg and I went to the Copenhagen poetry festival. It was raining heavily that day and we trudged through the mud of a distant suburb until we found the big tent in which the festival was being held. But in what sense could this be described as a poetry festival? In the midst of deafening rock music the poor poets scuttled up onto the stage like so many performing monkeys, looking hopeless down to their very postures, their voices totally muffled by the cacophony all round. When I looked more closely I could see the audience spread out on the ground swilling beer and smoking marijuana, bringing to mind Mayakovsky's famous line: "the sharp slap on the face administered by popular taste."

Poets have an extremely sensitive sixth sense, and are utterly without illusion as to whether they are making contact with their audience or not. Their minds are like parking garages: they know how many cars have come in and where they are parked, where there is damage and whether or not there are any oil leaks. Sometimes there is simply a void — the cars all drive through and go back out again.

Some languages are by their very nature suited for being read aloud. Many Russian poets recite as if they were in song, and even if you cannot understand what they are saying, you are still awed by the power of the voice. It must be said that China also had a tradition of such poetry recitals, but it was unfortunately lost some time ago.

There is nothing to be done about this, and who can imagine actually reciting new poetry in this way? At any rate, if we were to read poetry with the traditional rustic wail, we would not only drive away the audience, but summon the police, or at least any wild beasts that might be residing in the city.

Russian poetry provided the focus for the 1990 Rotterdam festival, and about a dozen Russian poets were invited to attend. The organizers had been warned about the poets, and took the precaution of locking the mini bars in their hotel rooms, but that didn't keep them from drinking. They had all gotten together and drunk more than their fair share before their readings began.

Bella Akhmadulina had been famous for her love poetry in the 1960s, and, while she had faded a good deal in the intervening years, she had been one of the Russian poets I had idolized at the time. We watched her stagger onto stage and stand still with great difficulty. But as soon as she opened her mouth her voice was extraordinary and the whole auditorium lit up. In that moment, and only in that moment, she was able to summon up the full measure of her earlier passion.

In the spring of 1990, I heard John Ashbery read in Stockholm while he was staggeringly drunk. His legs have problems to begin with, but on that day he was even more crippled, and walked as if he were negotiating a minefield.

The woman making the introductions added problems of her own, taking off her high heels as she walked across the stage. There ensued an odd dialogue between them — "Why did you take off your shoes?" "All the better to follow your poetry." Four years later I was on the same program with Ashbery, and there was some very good wine backstage. I asked him about the earlier occasion and he laughed, "I guess I do have a reputation." Even as he was saying this, he poured himself another generous glass.

Robert Bly recites as if he were conducting, his hands in constant motion as if the audience were a giant orchestra. Or you can also say, as if he were picking fruit, throwing out the bad and keeping the good (or the other way around). He is tall and stout with light flashing off his glasses; direct and optimistic by nature, he seems to correspond perfectly to the image of male power that he so readily advocates. When the two of us attended a poetry festival in Malmo in southern Sweden, I took him to the casino and taught him to play Twenty-one after our readings. After he returned to the U.S. he sent me a letter: "Writing poetry is like playing Twenty-one, most of the time you do no better than fifteen or sixteen."

Allen Ginsberg set many of his poems to music and would sing them while accompanying himself on a small gypsy accordion. Much of his fame rested on his recitations, and without them there would have been no Ginsberg and probably no Beat Generation. He was a master of rhyme and rhythm. While English is not as seemingly lyrical as Russian, its ever-changing rhythms can be combined with its rich slang and dialects to create a tongue especially suited for political condemnation. Thus are the ordinary people of no power or influence afforded the chance to let off some steam. When I read with Ginsberg at Eastern Michigan University, I was able to see how he controlled the audience. It was a kind of hypnosis: Allen had become a god, a foul-mouthed, angry god.

At Rotterdam, I ran into a true chanter of poetry from the Sahara. He had been intoning poetry most of his life, but they still gave him only twenty minutes on stage. He sat on a mat on the lounge floor, covered up tightly in his cape and talking to himself, sometimes soft, sometimes loud, perhaps governed by the noise of the blowing sands. He carried with him a small leather bag, which didn't contain poetry, but rather incantations and amulets with which, I thought, he would deal with the demonic society that limited his life to twenty minutes on stage. He had written most of his poems in the sand and they had been blown away by the wind, leaving only the sound, which endured as sturdily as the wind. He was full of admiration for the Chinese poet Ma Desheng who had read his poem that contained one hundred "fuckin's" that had stunned Paris.

While we were in Paris last autumn, we went to a coffee-house in a small suburban town to give a reading. It was raining that day but about twenty people showed up to hear us, which was more than we'd expected. That kind of evening was perfect for a reading, with the mesmerizing effect of wine combined with the sound of steady rain.

The last to recite was a French poet. He sighed and talked to himself with disjointed music made by shards of metal in the background. He took a paper package out of a bag and unwrapped it layer by layer, finally revealing a piece of raw beef. I grew wary as he rubbed his face with the raw beef and then commenced to roar into the microphone, making a deafening sound. I immediately plugged my ears, but still could sense his clamoring. Several frail older women made an escape, evidently fearing they would go deaf or undergo a stroke. He began to swallow the raw beef and almost choke on it. I began to fear that he might charge over and try to stuff into my mouth the piece of beef that he couldn't get down. His reading ended in hysterical roaring, his whole head covered in sweat and his face mottled like the piece of raw beef. I refused to shake hands with him, since, no matter how deep his message might have been, the noise he had made was an invasion of the existence of others.

Two years ago *The New York Times* Sunday magazine ran an article ridiculing American poets who depended upon giving readings to eat. When I think about it, I must be included in their number. The American system of higher education is different from the European in that it has creative writing programs, which have reading series attached to them. Poets thus become like monks, who need a temple to serve as a base from which they can fan out to the four quarters, content with a bottle and a begging bowl. As far as I know, there are few American poets not associated with their own "temple." Even Allen was unable to hold out becoming incorporated in the system he hated so much. Gregory Corso drifted in, but because of unseemly behavior, was driven right back out again. For poets, this is a question of to be or not . . .

Sometimes I grow weary when facing an audience. How did our predecessors recite poetry? Raising a cup to the wind, writing verse linked with others, presenting one's sharp feelings on the departure of a friend, birth and death without end.